No-Miss Lessons for PreTeen Kids 2

Group

Loveland, Colorado

Group's R.E.A.L. Guarantee to you:

Every Group resource incorporates our R.E.A.L. approach to ministry—a unique philosophy that results in long-term retention and life transformation. It's ministry that's:

This is EARL.
He's R.E.A.L.
mixed up.
(Get it?)

Relational
Because student-to-student interaction enhances learning and builds Christian friendships.

Experiential
Because what students experience sticks with them up to 9 times longer than what they simply hear or read.

Applicable
Because the aim of Christian education is to be both hearers and doers of the Word.

Learner-based
Because students learn more and retain it longer when the process is designed according to how they learn best.

No-Miss Lessons for Preteen Kids 2

Copyright © 2001 Group Publishing, Inc.

Visit our Web site: **www.grouppublishing.com**

Credits
Contributing Authors: Tim Baker, Trudy Hewitt, Karl Leuthauser, Kristi Rector, Donna K. Stearns, William Timothy Steed, and Paul Woods
Editors: Vicki L.O. Witte and Jim Hawley
Senior Editor: Karl Leuthauser
Chief Creative Officer: Joani Schultz
Copy Editor: Dena Twinem
Art Director: Kari K. Monson
Cover Art Director: Jeff A. Storm
Cover Designer: Alan Furst
Computer Graphic Artist: Tracy K. Donaldson
Cover Photographer: Daniel Treat
Illustrator: Gary Templin
Production Manager: Peggy Naylor

Library of Congress Cataloging-in-Publication Data
No-miss lessons for preteen kids 2 / [from the editors of] Group Publishing.
    p. cm.
  ISBN 0-7644-2290-1
   1. Christian education of children. 2. Church work with children.
 3. Children—Religious life. 4. Children—Conduct of life.
I. Group Publishing.
BV1475.2.N6 1997
268'.432—dc20

96-35339
CIP

10 9 8 7 6 5 4 3   10 09 08 07 06 05 04

Printed in the United States of America

Contents

Introduction

Section 1—What Is Faith?

Section 2—What's a Friend?

Section 3—All in My Family

Section 4—My Constantly Changing World

Section 5—Committed to Christ

Bonus Section—Committed to Serve

Introduction

Are your kids tired of studying the same old Bible stories in the same old ways? Are they ready to deepen their faith and take the challenge of living it out every day? If so, then *No-Miss Lessons for Preteen Kids 2* is for you!

A sequel to the popular *No-Miss Lessons for Preteen Kids*, this book offers lessons on relevant topics that challenge your kids, grow their faith, and give them practical ideas for living out their faith in meaningful ways. The special Bonus Section includes a lesson on sharing your faith, plus thirteen can't-miss service-project ideas your kids will love.

Lessons cover basic faith foundations such as God, Jesus, the Holy Spirit, and the church. When kids are sure of what their faith means in these areas, anything can happen!

Lessons also cover a topic of utmost importance to your preteens—getting along with family and friends. Who can't use a little help in these areas?

And to keep on top of what's hottest and most relevant to your kids, you'll find the section "My Constantly Changing World," which includes lessons on the Internet and other media, among other powerful topics.

Finally, help your kids to deepen and strengthen their faith with lessons on being committed to Christ.

No-Miss Lessons for Preteen Kids 2 offers fun and interesting approaches to all of these important topics in an easy-to-teach format complete with options for you to customize the lessons to best fit your group.

So grab your preteen kids and dive in!

Section 1:
• • • • • • • • • •
What Is Faith?

Scripture
Verses:
....
Genesis 1:1-28; 2:2-7;
2 Corinthians 5:7; Hebrews
11:1, 6; 1 Peter 1:8-9

Leader Tip

For this lesson, a chalkboard and chalk or a white board and a marker can be used instead of newsprint taped to the wall and a marker. Just make sure that kids can all see what you write no matter which method you choose.

Who Is God?

Preteens can have difficulty understanding and believing in a God they can't physically see. They begin wanting to have proof of why something is good or right or real instead of just believing that it is because a parent or teacher said so. They are starting to become independent, and that includes having thoughts and beliefs that are their own, not something they inherited from a grown-up.

This lesson helps your preteens understand that even though they can't see God, they can believe in him with confidence. They'll also see that God has given us evidence of his existence.

Choose Your Opening

Option 1: Do You Have to See It to Believe It?

(For this activity you'll need the video The Santa Clause *starring Tim Allen* (Walt Disney, PG), *newsprint, tape, and a marker.)*

Begin the lesson by showing a movie clip from *The Santa Clause*. Play the scene beginning approximately fifty minutes into the movie. This clip shows stepfather Neil asking Charlie how he knows that Santa Claus exists. The clip is about one minute long, and contains the phrase, "Just because you haven't seen it, doesn't mean it doesn't exist."

After showing the clip, tape a piece of newsprint up on the wall or use a chalkboard or white board to record students' answers. Write the words "Wind," "A million dollars," "Oxygen in the air," and "People in African jungle villages." Ask:

• **Can we all agree that these things exist in the world?**

After students respond affirmatively, say: **Let's look at each of these things one at a time. These are all things that we know exist, but we probably haven't seen. What evidence do we have that they exist?** For each one, ask kids to give reasons why they know these things exist, even if they've never seen them or can't see them. They might say they've seen pictures of African people, they've read about someone with a million dollars, or scientists can measure the wind or the oxygen in the air.

Option 2: Who Made It?

(For this activity you'll need enough books and pieces of fabric for each group to have one, homemade cookies or some other homemade treat, a paper bag with some leaves, flowers, sticks, grass, or other items you can find in nature, a piece of newsprint hung on the wall, and a marker.)

Divide kids into groups of three or four. Give each group a piece of fabric, some cookies (enough for each person to have one), and a book. Tell the groups that you'll give them two minutes for each object. During that time, they should investigate the object and come up with ways they know it is real.

After time is up, ask group members to call out reasons why they think the objects are real. Write their answers on the newsprint.

Then say: **Well, you've convinced me! These things must be real because** [state two or three reasons the students listed, such as they can see it, taste it, or they can physically manipulate the object]. Ask:

• **Did these things just come into existence on their own?**

When kids say no, ask:

• **Then how did they come into being for us to have here today?** Let kids give reasons until a student suggests that someone or something made the objects. Then pull out of the bag some leaves, flowers, sticks, or other objects from nature, and show them to the kids.

Say: **I guess someone or something had to have made these things, too.** Ask:

• **Who do you think made them?**

When students answer that God made the items, say: **If God made these things I'm holding, then he must be real and alive. But let's see what the Bible says.**

The Bible Experience
Who God Is

(For this activity you'll need Bibles, newsprint, and a marker.)

Say: **Believing in something we can't see takes faith. But we don't just believe in God blindly. He gives us much evidence to prove he exists. Let's look at two ways we can know God is real.**

Divide your class into groups of three to five, depending on class size, and assign each group one of the passages below. If you have a large class, you can assign the same verse to more than one group.

Verses: 2 Corinthians 5:7; Hebrews 11:1; Hebrews 11:6; 1 Peter 1:8-9.

Say: **One way we can know God is real is through reading his Word. He tells us in the book he wrote for us that he does exist and that we must have faith to believe him.** Give each group three minutes to read the passage and discuss how it proves that God is real. Then have each group report its answer to the class.

Say: **Another way we can know that God exists is by seeing what he has created. Let's look at some verses that tell us what we can see to know that God is real, even if we can't physically see him.**

Again, assign each group a Scripture passage to study, looking for physical evidence of God's existence.

Verses: Genesis 1:1-10; Genesis 1:11-19; Genesis 1:20-28; Genesis 2:2-7.

After groups have read the Scripture passages, have them call out things the verses say God made that we can see. Write the responses for everyone to see on the newsprint. Say: **Wow! God sure made a lot. And we can see things every day that remind us of God's creation and existence.**

I Believe

(For this activity copy and cut apart the "I Believe" handout found on page 9, making enough copies of the belief statement for each student to have one. You'll also need a pen or pencil for each student.)

Give an "I Believe" handout and a pen or pencil to each student. Together as a class, read the belief statement aloud in unison. Then ask everyone who believes the statement is true to sign it. Explain that no one will check to see if students signed the paper or not. Ask:

- **What might keep some people from signing this statement?**
- **What more might you or others need before you or they could sign this statement?**

Follow up with a prayer asking God to strengthen our faith and to open our eyes and hearts to the evidence he has given us for his existence.

Choose Your Closing

Option 1: All the Evidence

(For this activity you'll need a copy of the 4Him CD The Message, *and a CD player.)*

Play the song "All the Evidence I Need," from the 4Him CD *The Message*, which talks about walking by faith, not by sight, and trusting in invisible things. Ask:

- **What do you think it means that "the proof is living inside of me"?**
- **What evidence does this song offer for God's existence?**

Close class with prayer, giving students an opportunity to thank God for telling us about himself, and asking him to help them have faith and believe in him even though they can't see him.

Option 2: The Nature of Things

(For this activity you'll need leaves, flowers, or similar items, enough for one per student.)

Place the leaves and flowers spread out on a table and allow each student to choose one to keep. Say: **This will be a reminder that God is real and that he gives us evidence of his existence in the world around us.**

Explain to your students how they can press their leaves and flowers: Sandwich the object between layers of waxed paper and place on a level surface, such as a table or the floor. Then place several heavy books on top. Leave the leaf or flower there for several days; when it is dry, display it someplace where it can be seen often.

Close class with a prayer thanking God for making himself real to us and for showing us evidence of his existence.

I Believe

I believe that God is real.
I believe he gives me proof in the world around me that he exists.
I believe the Bible tells me that God is real, and that the Bible is true.
I believe in God even though I can't see him face to face.

Signed _____

Date_____

I Believe

I believe that God is real.
I believe he gives me proof in the world around me that he exists.
I believe the Bible tells me that God is real, and that the Bible is true.
I believe in God even though I can't see him face-to-face.

Signed _____

Date_____

I Believe

I believe that God is real.
I believe he gives me proof in the world around me that he exists.
I believe the Bible tells me that God is real, and that the Bible is true.
I believe in God even though I can't see him face-to-face.

Signed _____

Date_____

Scripture Verses:

Matthew 11:28-39; Luke 7:44-49; John 1:1-18; 3:16-17; Acts 9:34; Romans 5:8; 12:6a; 2 Corinthians 3:4; Hebrews 13:6; 1 Peter 1:13

Leader Tip

One way to find a piece of cardboard large enough for this activity is to break down a large appliance box.

Why Jesus?

Preteen kids want to know more about Jesus. They're beginning to look for more proof of his existence. And they're about to enter junior high—a tough time when they'll be faced with needing more than just a "Because mom and dad say so" understanding of Jesus.

Preteen kids need to know that Jesus heals their hurts, comforts them when friendships fail, and gives them gifts for use in his body. Jesus saved them, and he wants a relationship with them. He wants to be there when they need him, and when they think they don't. Help kids understand that Jesus is everything they could ever hope for, and everything they'll ever need.

Choose Your Opening
....

Option 1: Finding an Island

(For this activity you'll need a large piece of cardboard, plastic trash bags, and candy.)

Before the lesson place a large piece of cardboard in the center of the classroom. Make sure that the cardboard is just big enough for your entire class to fit standing on it. Place enough candy on the cardboard for each student to have one piece.

When kids arrive, have them get in groups of four. Give each group a plastic trash bag. Say: **You'll never believe this; the strangest thing has happened. The *entire* earth has been covered with water. The entire population of the world has been searching for the one piece of dry land, just so they can dry off and relax for a moment. Well, your groups are the only lucky ones who have found the one piece of dry land on the entire earth. It used to be a candy factory. You've got to move your group on a raft (the plastic trash bags) to the dry land. When you get to the land, you can move from your raft to the island. But here's the problem. You can't put your hands in the water—or touch the floor—because there are sharks. So the island's in sight, and you've got to get there. You can use whatever you want to get to the island as long as you stay on your raft.**

Instruct groups to start at the walls of the meeting room, and ask them not to put their hands in the water (touch the floor). Give groups time to move themselves to the dry land. Encourage students to be creative in their attempts to get their entire group to the island. Many groups will not be able to get to the island. Allow students to struggle with this, then after a few minutes, ask them to stop. Ask:

• **How does it feel knowing that you're close to the "dry land" but unable to get to it?**

• **When have you felt deprived of something you felt you absolutely needed?**

• **If I allowed you to put your hands "in the water," how quickly do you think you'd be able to get to the island?**

Tap your hand on the floor several times and tell kids that you've just put shark repellent in the water and it's now safe for them to put their hands in the water. Tell students that they can have one piece of candy when they reach the island. When all students are on the island, allow them to eat their candy.

Say: **Today we're going to talk about how we all need Jesus. Finding him is like finding the one island in the world. Let's look at why we need him.**

Option 2: My Whys

(For this activity you'll need index cards and pens or pencils.)

Have kids get in pairs and give each pair several index cards. Say: **Have you ever had one of those really big "why" questions that you could never get an answer to? Well, today we're going to talk about those questions. I'd like you to think of as many of those "why" types of questions as you can, and write each one on an index card. Two examples of a "why" question might be, "Why is the sky blue?" or "Why is it important to go to school?"**

Give kids time to write out their questions. Instruct pairs to make a distinctive mark on the back of their cards so they'll know which ones are theirs. As they finish, have students hand their questions to you. When everyone has finished, mix up the cards and make a neat pile. Say: **Now we're going to see how smart you are. I'd like you to come forward and take as many cards as you put in the stack, but don't take your own cards. Then I'd like you to work with your partner to give each question you read your best answer. You might not know what the answer is, but give one you think might be close. If you have no idea what the answer is, give a really funny answer.**

Give students time to write out their answers. As they finish, have students lay their cards face down on the floor at your feet. Instruct students to come forward to pick up their own question cards and read them. Ask:

• **What answers did you get that were funny?**

• **What answers did you get that you know are wrong?**

Say: **Today we're going to discuss one of the most difficult questions ever: Why should we trust in Jesus?**

The Bible Experience
....
The Jesus Experience

(For this activity you'll need a Bible, newsprint, and a marker for each group of three students.)

Have kids form groups of three. Give each group a Bible, a sheet of newsprint, and a marker. Say: **It's extremely important to understand who Jesus is. We have to know who he is before we can fully understand why we need him. So I'd like you to look at what the Bible says about who Jesus is.**

Instruct groups to read John 1:1-18. As they read, ask students to write down words and phrases that describe who Jesus is. When they're finished, have students gather in the center of the classroom.

Say: **Now that you've read about who he is, I'd like you to do your best at describing Jesus. Imagine that you're traveling to another planet to tell them about our world. You're part of the religious contingent of the crew. Your job is to tell the creatures on the other planet about Jesus. Please use only what you've discovered from reading the passage you just read.**

Give kids time to think of a few things to say. When they're ready, have trios come forward and share some of the things they might say to the aliens.

When kids are finished, ask:

• **What have you learned about Jesus from this?**

• **What does it mean that Jesus left his home in heaven and came to live with us?**

Read aloud John 3:16-17. Then say: **God loved us so much that he sent his Son to come and die for us. He did this because he loves us.**

Reflection and Application
All That He Does

(For this activity, photocopy and cut apart the "Who Needs Jesus?" cards (p. 14). You'll also need Bibles.)

Have students sit in a circle in the center of the classroom. Say: **We've seen where Jesus came from, and we've learned a little about his background. Now let's look at why exactly we need Jesus. I'm going to place eight cards face down in the center of the circle. I'd like one of you to take a card and read aloud what it says, then read aloud the Bible verse that's on the card.**

Have the first student read a card and the verse aloud. When he or she is finished, have another student pick another card and repeat the step. Continue until all of the cards and passages have been read. When students are finished reading, ask:

• **What are some other things that Jesus does that we didn't talk about?**

• **What have you learned about Jesus from reading these passages?**

• **How does knowing about Jesus and what he does for us make you feel?**

• **What decisions do we have to make based on what we've learned so far today?**

Say: **Jesus is really who the Bible says he is. We can trust God's Word. And we can rely on Jesus to help us in our lives.**

Choose Your Closing
Option 1: Who I Know

(For this activity you'll need index cards and pens or pencils.)

Say: **Think about everything that we've learned about Jesus today. We've discovered who he is, and we've discovered what he does in our lives.** Ask:

• **What sort of changes does Jesus make in our lives?**

• **Why do we need to make a decision to have a relationship with Jesus?**

• **What happens when we make a decision to have a relationship with Jesus?**

Say: **Jesus longs to have a relationship with us. We don't always feel like we're in touch with God. I'd like us to think about where we are in our relationship with God right now.**

Give each student an index card and a pen. Have preteens write on their cards how they feel about their relationship with Jesus.

Say: **We each have a unique relationship with Jesus. Some of you may have known Jesus for years, others may be new to having a relationship with him, and some of you may be seeking to know what a relationship with Jesus means. Wherever we are in our relationship with Jesus, we can be thankful. Let's pray and thank Jesus for this.**

Close the meeting with a prayer thanking Jesus for the opportunity to have a relationship with him.

Option 2: My Salvation

(Note: Use this closing option if you used the "My Whys" opening activity option. For this activity you'll need index cards and markers.)

Say: **At the beginning of this lesson, I asked you to think about the questions that you had in your life. Now I'd like to ask you a bigger question. If I were to ask you the big question, "Do you know this Jesus that we're talking about today?" what would you say?**

Give each student an index card and a marker, and have kids find a place in the meeting room where they can be alone. Ask students to respond to the question by writing either a "Yes" or a "No" on their index cards. When they're finished, have kids bow their heads and close their eyes. Then ask kids to hold their answers facing you so you can see them. Remind students to all keep their eyes closed. When students are finished, ask them to fold their cards so no one can see them.

Say: **God longs to have a relationship with us. Not one in which we say a prayer and then ignore him for the rest of our lives. Rather, he longs to talk with us, have us spend time in his Word, and get to know him. Let's close with prayer and thank God for sending Jesus.**

Close the meeting with a short prayer thanking God for sending Jesus. After the meeting, talk to the students who said that they don't have a relationship with Jesus.

Leader Tip

Make sure students know they can speak with you after class if they have further questions regarding their relationship with Jesus.

Who Needs Jesus?

Photocopy this handout, cut apart the cards, and place them in the center of the circle.

Jesus helps us—Hebrews 13:6

Jesus comforts us—Matthew 11:28-29

Jesus heals us—Acts 9:34

Jesus forgives us—Luke 7:44-49

Jesus gives us confidence—2 Corinthians 3:4

Jesus gives us hope—1 Peter 1:13

Jesus died for us—Romans 5:8

Jesus gives us gifts—Romans 12:6a

Who's Talking?

Goal:

To listen to the Holy Spirit's voice for guidance.

Scripture Verses:

John 14:26; 15:26; 16:13-14; Romans 8:8-9, 14

Television, computer games, peers, and even teachers bombard preteens with constant noise and stimulation. Is it any wonder our kids learn early to tune out and hear only what they want to hear?

Kids need to learn how to listen and what to listen to if they are to grow up making decisions that will lead them in God's path. Encourage your preteen kids to practice listening to the Holy Spirit. When they face decisions that will affect their future, they will recognize God's guidance in their lives.

Choose Your Opening

Option 1: Do You Hear What I Hear?

(For this activity provide a piece of paper and pencil for each group.)

After kids arrive, form groups of two or three and give each group a piece of paper and a pencil. Say: **Today we're going to discover how many sounds are in our world. Go with your group outside and list all the different sounds you hear. You will have sixty seconds to record all you hear. More instructions will follow.**

Follow the group outdoors. Say quietly: **List your sounds in alphabetical order. Number your sounds as you hear them.** After sixty seconds, call the groups back inside. Ask for a volunteer from one group to report what sounds the group heard. Ask the other groups for any different sounds they heard.

Ask:

• **Did anyone hear a sound they didn't recognize?**

• **Did everyone hear the instructions I gave outside? What were they?**

• **Did you learn anything about yourself or this world through this exercise?**

After a few preteens offer their thoughts, say: **There's a lot of noise in our world. Sometimes the noise and busyness of life causes us to miss the really important things. Today, we're going to talk about listening to and recognizing a sound you may or may not be familiar with...the voice of God.**

Option 2: Who's That Anyway?

(For this activity you'll need a tape recorder, a blank tape, and an adult or teen volunteer to do some voice impersonations.)

Before class ask an adult or teen volunteer to help you make a tape of three or four voice impersonations of famous people or people from your church. For example, they could impersonate the pastor, the song leader, Elvis Presley, or Bugs Bunny.

It's not as important for your volunteer to sound exactly like the person as it is for him or her to use words or phrases the kids can recognize as belonging to that person. For example, if you're going to have someone impersonate Bugs Bunny, you might have him or her say, "What's up, Doc?"

After kids arrive, form four groups. Tell them you are going to play a game called, "Who's That Anyway?" Say: **You will hear four different impersonations. After each one I will give a group fifteen seconds to guess who the person is. If that group is wrong, the next group will guess. Each group will get to listen to a different impersonation. The group with the most points will get to do an impersonation for the rest of us.**

After the game, ask:

• **Who was the voice behind the impersonation?**

• **What made it hard or easy to recognize the voice?**

• **What made it hard or easy to recognize the person being impersonated?**

Say: **God speaks to us in many ways to guide us in the choices we face each day. One of the main ways is through his Holy Spirit. Today we're going to learn how to recognize God's Holy Spirit when he directs us.**

The Bible Experience
....

The Holy Spirit

(For this activity, provide a Bible, a permanent marker or medium-point ballpoint pen, and one large balloon with "John 14:26," "John 15:26," and "John 16:13-14" written on it for every four people. You will also need a large sheet of newsprint, marker, and tape.)

Create a large speech balloon (like the ones used for cartoons) from a sheet of newsprint and tape it to the wall. Form groups of four. Give each group a Bible, a marker or pen, and a balloon. Say: **How many of you have seen the speech balloons used in comics? Today we're going to make speech balloons—except we're going to use real balloons. When your group blows up your balloon, you'll find some Bible verses written on it. Take turns looking up the verses and reading them to your group. As you read each verse, talk about what you learn about the Holy Spirit. Write in as few words as possible on your balloon what you learn about the Holy Spirit from the verses.**

While groups are working, tape the large newsprint speech balloon on the wall. After groups finish, ask for a volunteer from each group to bring his or her group's balloon and tape it beside the newsprint speech balloon. Ask the volunteer to write one thing his or her group discovered about the Holy Spirit on the speech balloon. Each group should write something different. If any group has other things not listed, allow a volunteer to write them on the newsprint.

Say: **The verses we just read tell us that the Holy Spirit is our counselor and our guide. He teaches us about Jesus and shows us how to live in a way that honors God. The verses also show us that those who believe in Jesus have the Holy Spirit to guide them. Look at the speech balloon we created.**

Ask:

- How does the Holy Spirit do each of the things we listed?
- How does the Holy Spirit communicate his direction and guidance for our lives?
- Does God talk to people? If so, what does he sound like?

Say: **The Holy Spirit guides and directs us in many different ways. The first place to look for God's direction is in the Bible. If the direction we're getting doesn't match up with the rest of the words the Holy Spirit has given in the Bible, you can be sure it's not God's direction. The Holy Spirit also guides us through the people he's put in our lives—like our parents, Sunday school teachers, and pastors. Sometimes the Holy Spirit directs us through circumstances. The Holy Spirit also directly leads us. When you ask God for direction, don't expect to hear an audible voice. Instead, expect to get an impression and a feeling in your heart about what is right and what you should do. Our own feelings and thoughts can mislead us. But if you really try to follow God's leading and accept whatever direction the Holy Spirit gives, he will lead you.**

Reflection and Application
Who's in Control?

(For this activity copy and cut apart the "Who's in Control?" handout on page 19. You'll also need a Bible.)

Divide your group in half. Place the "Who's in Control?" situations from the handout between the two groups.

Say: **It's not always easy to know what's right or wrong. If we learn to follow the Holy Spirit's direction, we will always be led in the right way. A volunteer will choose a situation from the stack and read it aloud. His or her group will then decide if the person's response shows a willingness to follow the Holy Spirit or to follow our sinful nature.**

The other group will then decide to agree or disagree and tell how the person in the situation could have otherwise responded. If you believe the person did follow the Holy Spirit's direction, tell what could have happened if the person rejected the Holy Spirit's direction. If you believe the person didn't follow the Holy Spirit's direction, explain what could have happened if the person followed the Holy Spirit's leading.

Ask for a volunteer to begin. Give kids in both groups the opportunity to be readers. Allow kids to share their ideas freely.

After the four situations are explored, read Romans 8:8-9, 14 and say: **God gives those who believe in Jesus his Holy Spirit to lead them in his way. Sometimes we forget to listen to the Holy Spirit and choose wrong things. That's why we need to learn to listen to him so we can make choices that are pleasing to God.**

Option 1: Put It in Action

(For this activity you will need Bibles, concordances, paper, and pencils.)

Have kids form trios, and hand out paper and pencils to students. Say: **We've talked a bit about what the Holy Spirit does and how he guides us. Now I'd like us to put it into practice. I'd like each person to share one thing you need the Holy Spirit's direction for. As a group, pray together and ask for the Holy Spirit's help. Then use the concordance and Bible to find verses that apply to your situation. Write down the verses to take home for future reference. When you're done looking for the verses, spend some more time praying with your group and talking about where the Holy Spirit is directing you. Make sure each person has a chance to bring up an issue.**

While kids work, monitor the group, helping kids use the concordances and redirecting non-biblical advice or decisions. Then allow volunteers to share the issues they prayed about and the direction they plan to take.

Option 2: Which Way?

(For this activity you'll need a pencil and a piece of paper for each person.)

Give each student a piece of paper and a pencil. Ask the kids to choose a partner. Say: **We've discussed how to face some tough decisions. Perhaps you're facing a difficult decision right now. I want each of you to write down a decision you have faced or are facing. Don't put your name on the paper because I will read these aloud later.** (If kids need help thinking of something, remind them again of the decisions from the "Who's in Control?" activity.)

After a few minutes, pass a container around for the kids to drop their papers in. Say: **I'm going to draw out a paper and read it aloud. After I read it, turn to your partner and discuss how the Holy Spirit could help this person decide what to do.**

After the kids share, ask them to discuss their answers with the class. Read as many of the papers as you have time for.

Close by having the kids form a circle and join hands. Ask each one to thank God for sending his Holy Spirit to guide them.

Who's in Control?

1. You've studied these spelling words a hundred times, but you're blank on this one word. You decide to leave the answer blank, but as you stand to hand in your paper, you see the correct answer on a friend's paper. Quickly, you sit back down and write it in. You know it's OK to do because you studied so hard.

2. You join a group of your friends at school. You're all laughing and joking around. Suddenly, the laughter stops. You turn to see what's caught everyone's attention. You roll your eyes. It's "Smelly Shelly." She never takes a bath and she's headed your way. She calls out to the group, but they turn and start down the hallway. You act like you didn't hear her and walk away too. You feel bad inside but hey, it's her fault. She could take a bath.

3. You look at the five dollars on the table. Your mom already gave you money to give to the Sunday school hunger drive. But you spent it at the arcade. Now, you have to go to class empty-handed...or maybe not. God probably had somebody leave that money on the table knowing it would go for a good cause. As you pick up the five dollars, you think about how good it is for God to provide.

4. You sit down at the computer and click onto the Internet. Mom and Dad are outside. Accidentally, you click onto a site you know you shouldn't be at. You start to close the site, but one of the pictures catches your attention. You scroll on down, and down a little further. Suddenly, you hear the back door. Quickly, you get out of the site and click on a game. When your mom asks you what you're doing, you tell her that you're playing computer games. The youth group meeting suddenly pops into your mind. It was about honoring your parents. You decide to talk to your mom and tell her exactly what happened.

Goal:
To learn, worship, share, and pray with others in church.

Scripture Verses:
Acts 2:41-47

Why Church?

As preteens move from concrete thinking to more abstract reasoning, they start the process of questioning their beliefs. This process is a normal part of seeking to understand and personalize their faith. In this lesson, students will explore the question, "Why Church?" The goal of this study is to help preteens discover the purpose of the local church, and to respond in worship to God and service to God and others.

Choose Your Opening

Option 1: Human Knot

(For this activity you will not need any supplies.)

Have all of your students stand in a circle. If you have more than ten students in your class, divide into groups of eight to ten. If your class is small, you may join them for this activity. Say: **Today we are going to start with an activity that will require everyone to work together. There's no succeeding on your own in this activity; you will have to communicate with, listen to, and cooperate with each other.**

Direct your students to stretch out their arms, and to grasp hands with two other people. Everyone should have somebody else's hands in each of their own hands, but no two people should be holding only each other's hands. At this point your group should resemble a giant human knot.

Give your students these instructions: **Your job is to untie this knot. Here is the only rule: You must keep your hands held together—no letting go. That's it. Work together to get yourselves untied.**

Watch your students as they work together to untangle themselves. If you have more than one group, be sure to circulate and check on each group's progress. Resist the urge to offer suggestions, and let your students work out this puzzle on their own.

When your students have finally untied themselves, they should all be standing in a circle again, still holding hands. Congratulate them, and debrief with these questions:

- **What was the hardest part of this activity?**
- **What was the most fun?**
- **What was absolutely necessary in this activity?**
- **How is this like church?**

Direct students to see that in church we are all supposed to be working toward the same goal, but we might have different ideas about how to get there. We all need to work together, to listen to each other, and to cooperate.

Option 2: Design a Church

(For this activity you will need pencils and a copy of the "New Church Committee Report" handout on page 24 for each group.)

Form groups of three. Give each group a copy of the "New Church Committee Report" handout. Say: **We are going to use our imaginations today. Imagine that our church has decided to start a new church in a nearby community. You are part of the committee that will help get this new church going. Your committee will decide the name of the new church, what activities you would like the church to do, and the schedule for the Sunday morning service. I have given each group a handout with all the information you need to complete your committee's report. Elect one of your members to write down your committee's ideas. This activity is a lot of fun, but try to keep your answers on the handout serious.**

Give your students about fifteen minutes for this activity. When they have finished, ask one volunteer from each group to share their results with the class. Then say: **In chapter two of the book of Acts, the disciples started the very first church. Let's look at what the church of Jerusalem did together.**

The Bible Experience
The Church: Going and Growing

(For this activity you will need a Bible, a pencil, and paper for each person. You'll also need a white board and marker, or chalkboard and chalk.)

Give students Bibles, pencils, and paper. You can have your kids do this activity individually, or you may want to have them get into groups of two or three. Tell your students: **Read Acts 2:41-47, then make a list of everything this passage says the early church did together.** When they're finished, have your kids share what they discovered from the Scripture, while you write their responses on the board.

Say: **We can see from Acts 2:41-47 that the early church did many things together. We can summarize their activities with four words: learning, worshipping, sharing, and praying.** Write these four words on the board. **Can you pick one item you wrote down from Acts 2 and tell us which of the four words on our board relates to that item?**

After they have responded, say: **The first church was a place of learning, worshipping, sharing, and prayer. I think these four activities tell us why we have churches. The purpose of the church is to learn, worship, share, and pray.**

Reflection and Application
How Do We Rate?

(For this activity you will need a white board and a marker.)

Tell your students: **The church is to be a place for learning, worship, sharing, and prayer. Let's look now at our church and see how you think our church rates in those four areas.** Have your students look back to the white board where you wrote the words "learning," "worshipping," "sharing," and "praying." Ask:

- **Which one of the four areas do you think our church does the best?**
- **Which one of the four areas do you think our church needs to improve?**
- **Which one of the four areas do you think our class does the best?**
- **Which one of the four areas do you think our class needs to improve?**

Tell your students: **These four things are essential to a church that wants to grow. They are also essential for any Christian who wants to grow closer to Christ.** Ask:

- **Which one of the four areas do you think you do well?**
- **Which one of the four areas do you think you need to improve?**

Choose Your Closing

Option 1: Improve Your Rating

(For this activity you will need a white board and a marker.)

Refer back to your white board on which the words "learning," "worshipping," "sharing," and "praying" are written. Write students' responses to the following questions. Ask:

- **If a person felt that he or she needed to learn more about God or his Word, what could that person do?**
- **If a person felt that he or she needed to worship more or differently, what could that person do?**
- **If a person felt that he or she needed to share more with other Christians, what could that person do?**
- **If a person felt that he or she needed to pray more, what could that person do?**

Then ask your students:

- **What specifically can you do to improve one of the following areas in your own life: learning, worship, sharing, or prayer?**

After they have shared, close by praying for your preteens as they seek to grow closer to Christ.

Option 2: Leader Interview

(For this activity arrange for several lay leaders or pastors from your church to drop by at the end of your class time.)

Tell your students: **Today we have discovered the reasons or goals for the church. In a moment a few of the people who minister in our church are going to join us. We are going to have the opportunity to interview them and find out what they do for our church. But before they join us, let's think of some questions we might want to ask them.**

Brainstorm with your kids what questions they want to ask. If they need some help getting started, suggest some questions such as these:

- **What do you do for our church?**

• **How do you work together with other people in our church?**

• **How does your job fit into one of these categories of goals for the church: learning, worshipping, sharing, praying?**

• **What are some ways that kids like us can help our church achieve its goals?**

When your group has finished interviewing the leaders, pray for the leaders or have your students pray for them. Pray also for your kids as they take up their roles within the church.

Leader Tip

If you can't interview any of your church's leaders, your kids might want to send thank-you notes to a few of the volunteers in your church. Get the names of some volunteers before class.

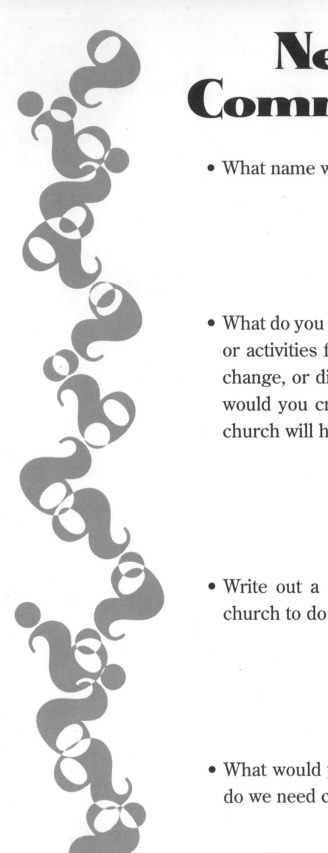

New Church Committee Report

- What name would you like to give your new church?

- What do you want your new church to do? What ministries or activities from our old church would you like to keep, change, or discontinue? What new ministries or activities would you create? Write down what ministries your new church will have.

- Write out a schedule of what you would like your new church to do when it meets for Sunday morning worship.

- What would you say is the goal of this new church? Why do we need churches?

Section 2:
• • • • • • • • • •
What's a Friend?

Scripture
Verses:
....
Ruth 1:1-18; Proverbs
17:17a; 18:24b; 27:10;
John 15:13-17

Being a Friend

Preteen kids change "best" friends almost as often as they change their clothes. This is the time in their lives when they need to develop good, lasting friendships that will help them through the trials of the coming years. In order to do this, preteens need to understand that the cement of friendship involves a commitment that doesn't change with every disagreement or bad time friends may face.

Choose Your Opening

Option 1: Famous Friends

(For this activity you will need enough copies, cut apart, of the "Famous Friends" handout on page 30 to give a name to each kid in your class.)

After students arrive, give them each a name from the "Famous Friends" list. Tell kids not to look at the name until you have given all of the instructions. Say: **Each of you has a name. The name is half of a famous friendship. When I say "go," you will have two minutes to find the other half that completes the famous friendship. Sound easy? I thought so too. So, to make it harder, you cannot tell anyone who you are, or the name of the friend you are looking for. You can only give hints to these names. For example, if my name were "Beauty," I could say I'm from a famous cartoon movie and I'm looking for a big hairy creature to be my prince. If the other person is the "Beast," he or she could say, "I'm that creature and you must be Beauty." If the other person isn't the Beast, you both have to keep looking. Go.**

After time is up, if any students still haven't found their friends, allow the kids to call out their names and find their friends. Ask:

• **What made it possible for these famous friends to remain friends?**

After some discussion, say: **These friends didn't always agree, nor did they like all the same things. Some even had other friends. But no matter what they faced or how they might have disagreed, they always stuck together. They knew they were stronger together than apart. Today we are going to explore some other famous friendships—friendships found in the Bible.**

Option 2: Sticking Together

(For this activity you will need a piece of Velcro, measuring at least an inch by an inch, and a fastener for every two people. The Velcro needs to have a sticky, self-adhesive back. You will also need a piece of bubble gum for each preteen.)

After all kids have arrived, count them off by fours. As you count them off, hand the ones and twos the top part of the Velcro and the threes and fours the bottom part of the Velcro. Tell the kids to stick their Velcro on their hands, shoulders, knees, or feet. Say: **Once your Velcro is on, don't take it off until the game is over. When I say "go," the Ones will have two minutes to find all the Threes and stick together. The Twos will have two minutes to find the Fours and stick together. The group with the most stuck together at the end of the two minutes wins. Go!**

At the end of the two minutes, call time and announce the winner. Say: **The winning team will get a piece of bubble gum because they stuck together so well. The other team will also get a piece because they need a little extra sticking power.**

After kids get "unstuck" and remove the Velcro from their hands or clothing, ask:

• **How was this game like friendship?** (Some possible answers: It's fun to have friends who stick with you; sometimes it's hard to stick by a friend; a real friend will stick by you even in a tough situation.)

Say: **Today we're going to look at some friends who had what it takes to stick together when things got tough.**

The Bible Experience

Friends Forever

(For this activity provide a pencil, paper, and a Bible for each group.)

Form three groups of one to six people each. If your class is large, form six groups, assigning two groups to the same passage of Scripture.

After forming groups, instruct the preteens to choose two people to read, one person to tell the class what happened in the Scripture or what it means, one to ask the questions, one to encourage everybody in the group to participate in answering the questions, and one person to report the group's findings to the rest of the class. The jobs can be combined in order to accommodate the number of students in your groups and in your class.

Group 1's Scripture: Ruth 1:1-18

Group 1's questions:

• **What problem did Ruth and Naomi face?**

• **How do you know they were friends?**

Group 2's Scripture: Proverbs 17:17a; 18:24b; 27:10

Group 2's questions:

• **What does a friend do at all times?**

• **What should you never do to a friend?**

Group 3's Scripture: John 15:13-17

Group 3's questions:

• **How did Jesus show us that he is a true friend?**

• **How can we show our friendship with Jesus?**

Leader Tip

Write the instructions on a piece of newsprint and hang on the wall to keep kids from repeatedly asking for directions. Or write instructions on a white board or chalkboard.

After groups have finished, allow each group to report their findings to the whole group. Say: **Ruth and Naomi proved their friendship even when things got tough. Ruth could have done as her sister-in-law, Orpah, did. She could have gone back to her own family and her own country as Naomi told her to. But Ruth loved Naomi and knew that she needed her. Naomi, on the other hand, could have begged Ruth to come with her, making her feel guilty for thinking about going back to her own home. But both loved each other and wanted the best for each other. They promised to stick together, to help each other, and that's what they did.**

Jesus gave us the ultimate example of friendship. He not only said that the true test of friendship is to lay down your life for your friend; he actually did it. Jesus literally gave up his life for us, proving his never-ending love for us.

Reflection and Application
Friends Forever

(For this activity you will need a copy of the "Forever Friends" worksheet on page 31 and a pencil for each person, plus a Bible for yourself.)

Read aloud Proverbs 17:17a; 18:24b; and 27:10. Say: **These verses tell us that a true friend loves all the time, sticks closer than a brother, and does not forsake his friends. Ruth and Naomi were true friends. Jesus is a true friend. How good a friend are you?**

Distribute the "Forever Friends" worksheet, one per student, and give your class a few minutes to complete the worksheet. Assure them that nobody needs to see their answers, and that they can answer using pictures or symbols if they prefer to ensure their privacy.

Choose Your Closing
Option 1: A Friend Like U

(Use this activity if you used the "Famous Friends" opening. For this activity you will need the song "A Friend Like U," from the CD Geoff Moore & The Distance Greatest Hits, *a CD player, and a copy of the lyrics on a large piece of newsprint. Each student will need paper and a pencil.)*

Play the song "A Friend Like U" for your class. Encourage your kids to sing along the second time through, and let them make up appropriate actions to go with the song.

Give each student a piece of paper and a pencil. Say: **Today we talked about some famous friends from cartoons and television. Then we discovered some famous friends in the Bible. These were real people with real problems and real feelings. Because Ruth and Naomi loved each other so much, they promised to be friends for life, and they showed they meant it by sticking together when things got tough. Today, I want you to write a letter to one of your friends. Tell your friend why he or she is special to you.**

After kids write their letters, have everyone join hands and close in prayer, thanking God for giving us good friends.

Option 2: Friendly Thoughts

(For this activity you will need a piece of poster board, old magazines, glue, scissors, and markers for each group.)

Have students work in groups. Ask one person in each group to write "A friend loves at all times (Proverbs 17:17a)" in the middle of the poster board. Say: **Ruth and Naomi shared a special friendship. So did Jesus and his disciples. Each person should look through the magazines and find five words and/or pictures that remind you of your friends. Cut them out and glue them to the poster board to make a collage.**

After the kids finish the collages, ask for volunteers to share why they chose the words or pictures they did. Then hang the collages around the room. Ask the kids to join hands and close in a prayer thanking God for giving us good friends.

Famous Friends

R2D2	C3PO
Charlie Brown	Snoopy
The Fox	The Hound
Fred	Barney
Mickey	Minnie
Simba	Nala
Timone	Pumba
Pebbles	Bam Bam
Batman	Robin

Forever Friends

How good a friend are you? Do you love at all times? Do you stick closer than a brother? Are you always loyal to your friends? Think about the following questions to help you evaluate where you need some work on being a better friend.

- When was the last time you ditched a friend or "stood up" a friend?

- When was the last time you stood up *for* a friend even though it might have made you look bad?

- When was the last time you insisted on your own way with a friend?

- When was the last time you did what your friend wanted to do, even though you had other ideas of your own?

- When was the last time you turned down spending time with a friend in order to do something else?

- When was the last time you chose to spend time with a friend rather than doing something else?

- How can you be a better friend?

Me Last!

Preteen kids are beginning to be incredibly self-absorbed. Some think the world revolves around them, everyone is looking at them, and their lives are constantly on review. They think everyone notices everything about them. If nobody notices them, that's even worse.

Help your kids realize that Jesus' ideas of how we think about ourselves and others are exactly opposite of how the world tells us to think. We are not to be selfish, but self-less.

Choose Your Opening
....

Option 1: Gospel or Garbage

(For this activity you will need a Bible.)

This is a game in which kids will get a chance to think about statements that relate to always wanting to have the best and to be first. You will need to move chairs so kids can move back and forth across the room freely.

Say: **This is a game in which you get to choose whether you think a statement is gospel or garbage. Statements that are gospel are from the Bible. Statements that are garbage might be kind of based on biblical instruction, but they're all twisted up, not the way the Bible says it at all.**

Everyone needs to stand. If you think the statement is gospel, move to the wall on my left. If you think it's garbage, move to the wall on my right.

Read each statement and have kids move to the side of the room that represents their opinion. Then tell them what the real answer is and read aloud the Bible verse that proves it.

1. Few things are impossible with God. (Garbage. Luke 1:37)

2. He has brought down rulers from their thrones but has lifted up the humble. (Gospel. Luke 1:52)

3. John the Baptist helped Jesus, and used to tie Jesus' sandals. (Garbage. John 1:27)

4. Everything is in Jesus' hands. (Gospel. John 3:35)

5. Jesus said we should always have the best spot at the table and the best seats in the house. (Garbage. Luke 11:43; 14:7-11)

6. Whoever is humble like a little child is the greatest in heaven. (Gospel. Matthew 18:4)

7. The last will be first and the first will be last. (Gospel. Matthew 20:16; Mark 9:35)

Option 2: Backward Relay

(For this activity you will need blindfolds.)

Have preteens form relay teams with up to five kids in each team. Have the first person in the line put on a blindfold. Designate a finish line. Say: **This relay is a little different. Each team needs to help its blindfolded team member complete the relay, by telling him or her the direction to move. When your team's player has returned to tag the next player, he or she must don the blindfold and follow the team's instructions.**

Have teams turn their runners around a few times. Make sure they are not pointing straight when you begin the game. When kids are finished with the relay, have them discuss:

• **How was this relay different from others you've done?**

• **When you were blindfolded, how did you have to depend on your team's help?**

• **When you were in line, how did you help your blindfolded teammate complete the relay?**

Say: **Usually when you run a relay, it's all up to the person who's running his or her leg of the relay. You don't need to think about your team members. But in this relay, you had to rely on your team members. Today we're going to talk about how we can think about others first.**

The Bible Experience

It's *Not* About Me!

(For this activity you will need Bibles.)

Ask:

• **What are the special meals that your family shares each year? Thanksgiving? Christmas? Birthdays?** Give plenty of time for kids to share.

Say: **Jesus shared a very important meal with his disciples. Let's turn in our Bibles to Luke 22:14-16 and read about it.** Have a volunteer read the passage aloud.

Jesus knew what was coming, and he planned a really important dinner. It would be his last meal with his disciples. That's why we call it the Last Supper. He had a lot of significant things he wanted to share with the disciples before the end of his life on earth. But instead of focusing on the coming crucifixion and resurrection, the disciples had some personal issues in mind. Let's look at verses 24-27 to see if you can tell what the disciples were most worried about.

Have a volunteer read these verses aloud. Ask:

• **What was it that the disciples were most worried about?**

• **When do we sometimes worry about being the best or being the first or having the best toy or best food or best place?**

• **Why is it hard, when we're concerned with other things, to think about what Jesus would want us to do?**

Say: **Just before this meal took place, Jesus gave us an example of what he would want us to do. I'm going to read John 13:1-16. It's a long passage. I want you to follow along in your Bibles, and look for the thing Jesus is telling us to do.**

Read the verses aloud. Give kids a chance to share what they think the answer is.

Say: **Jesus wants us to be servants. But can't that be a hard thing for us**

Extra! Extra!

To help illustrate how humans start out totally self-centered, show selected clips from any of the following videos: *Look Who's Talking, Honey I Blew up the Kid,* or even the scene from *The Prince of Egypt* in which Moses' mother puts him into the basket. Her heart is breaking, and he's oblivious. Also good are some of the clips from *The Lion, the Witch, and the Wardrobe* in which Edmund exhibits total disregard for the others in his desire for candy.

to do? When we're born, we're completely self-centered—as babies we're me-first people.

Ask:

• **Do you think Jesus wants us to be me-first people? Why?**

Say: **Jesus really wants us to become me-last people. That's what he was trying to show us here. Let's look at one more Scripture.**

Turn to Matthew 23:11-12. Read the verses aloud. Ask:

• **What does it mean to humble yourself?**

• **What is God telling us here about insisting on being first?**

• **Why do you think God would want us to be humble, to be second? Does that mean that he doesn't want us to do our best?**

Say: **God always wants us to do our best. So what is it that he doesn't want us to do? God doesn't want us to always try to get the best and be the first in line. He wants us to be humble. He wants us to serve others, and think of them before ourselves.**

Reflection and Application

Who, Me?

(For this activity you will need Bibles, pencils, and a copy of the "Who, Me?" worksheet on page 36 for each student.)

Say: **We're going to have some time now for personal reflection.** Have kids silently read Matthew 20:20-23, 26-28.

Pass out pencils and copies of the "Who, Me?" worksheet to each student.

Say: **Keeping your Bibles open to that story, use the "Who, Me?" worksheet I'm passing around to rate yourself on putting others first.**

Give kids enough time to finish the worksheets. You may let kids share answers, or simply let this be a time for personal reflection. When most kids have finished, move into the closing activity.

Choose Your Closing

Option 1: Journals

(For this activity you will need something that will work as a journal for each student. You might purchase small, simple notebooks, or just staple several pieces of paper together. You will also need pencils.)

Say: **Keeping a journal is one activity that often helps us keep track of how we're growing with God. Journals are great to look back through. It can be a growing experience to put down our thoughts on paper, and then go back weeks or months later and see where we used to be in our journey with God.**

I have some small journals here, and I'd like to ask you to begin to use them. Start by evaluating where you are on the topic of "Me Last!" I'd like to ask you to commit to doing this for fifteen days. You don't have to make long entries, but try to make honest ones.

Pass out the journals and pencils.

Say: **It's very important to write an entry every day. At the end of each day's entry, try to write a little prayer. Then you can go back and see how God answered those prayers. It's fun!**

Have your class begin writing their first journal entries now. Close class in prayer, asking God to help your class members remember to think of others before themselves.

Option 2: Cartoons

(For this activity you will need pencils and paper.)

Say: **We're going to create cartoons of what it might look like to be last instead of always trying to be first. The cartoons don't have to necessarily be funny, but they should illustrate what we've been learning. They also don't have to be artistic. Stick figures will work just fine.**

Distribute pencils and paper, and give kids a few minutes to work. When kids are finishing, let them share their cartoons with their classmates.

Close class in prayer, asking God to help your class members remember to think of others before themselves.

Who, Me?

On a scale of 1 to 10 (1 being lowest and 10 being highest) rate how you do putting others first in the following situations:

Lunch line at school

1   2   3   4   5   6   7   8   9   10

Cash register line

1   2   3   4   5   6   7   8   9   10

Choosing teams

1   2   3   4   5   6   7   8   9   10

Snacks at home

1   2   3   4   5   6   7   8   9   10

Using video games

1   2   3   4   5   6   7   8   9   10

Getting into car

1   2   3   4   5   6   7   8   9   10

Sharing with siblings

1   2   3   4   5   6   7   8   9   10

Extra Dinner Food

1   2   3   4   5   6   7   8   9   10

Playing sports

1   2   3   4   5   6   7   8   9   10

Forgiving Friends

Friendships are important to preteens. At this age, youth are beginning to learn that even close friends sometimes hurt each other. In order for preteens to continue to develop friendships and to stick with their friends, they must learn how to forgive. In this lesson, kids will learn that giving up revenge and choosing to do what is best for the other person are the most basic elements of forgiveness.

Choose Your Opening

Option 1: Snapped By a Friend

(For this activity you will need several rubber bands for each pair of students.)

Have students form teams of two people each. Give each pair one rubber band. Tell students: **We are going to have a contest to see which team can break its rubber band first. Both persons on the team should hold their team's rubber band by their index and middle fingers only. When I say "go," pull your band as far as you can until it snaps. The team that breaks its rubber band first wins.**

Try this contest several times. When you've finished, ask:

• **What happened when the rubber band broke?**

• **Who got snapped the most?**

• **After you got hurt by the rubber band, how did you feel about playing the game again with your partner?**

• **How is getting snapped by the rubber band similar to getting your feelings hurt by a friend?**

• **Without giving a name, can you tell us of a time when a friend hurt your feelings?**

Say: **Today we are going to learn what it means to forgive our friends when they have hurt us.**

Option 2: Musical Chairs

(For this activity you will need chairs, a musical CD, and a CD player.)

Begin your class time today with a whirlwind game of musical chairs. Arrange the chairs so that you have one chair fewer than you have students. Explain to students that they must walk around the group of chairs, and when you turn off the music they must sit down. The person left standing will be kicked out of the game, and must stand alone near one of the meeting room walls.

Start the music and the game, turning off the music only a few seconds after starting it. Continue at a whirlwind pace, disqualifying kids without listening to any arguments. Do not allow the kids who have been eliminated to speak to each other. When you have only one person left, congratulate the winner. Then ask:

- **How did it feel to be eliminated from the game?**
- **How did it feel not to be allowed to speak to anybody else that had been eliminated?**
- **How did it feel to play this game so quickly with no time for arguments?**
- **How is this game like being hurt or let down by a friend?**
- **How do you feel when a friend leaves you out or won't talk to you?**
- **Without giving a name, can you tell us of a time when a friend hurt your feelings?**

The Bible Experience

Payback or Pardon

(For this activity provide pencils, paper, and Bibles for each person. You will also need a white board and marker, or a chalkboard and chalk.)

Have kids form groups of two or three, and give each group Bibles, pencils, and paper. Have the students look up Romans 12:17-21 and follow along as you read the passage aloud. Say: **In this passage, Paul was talking about how to forgive someone who has hurt you. In your group, make a list of all the things Paul said we should *not* do when someone hurts us. Then make a second list of what he says we *should* do.**

When the groups have finished, have them share their results while you make a master list on the board. Answers might include the following: What we should *not* do—pay back evil for evil, take revenge, or be overcome by evil. What we *should* do—do what is right, live at peace with others, help them, and overcome evil with good.

Now have your students turn to Ephesians 4:32, and ask a volunteer to read the verse aloud. Ask:

- **What does Paul say here that we should do to those who hurt us? Why?**

Say: **Paul said that we should be kind and compassionate and forgive others, because God in Christ has forgiven us. Now you might think your friend has done some pretty rotten things to you, but just think for a minute about all the things God has forgiven us for. As a matter of fact, Jesus did not just suggest that we forgive others, he commanded it.**

Have your students turn to Matthew 6:14-15, and ask a volunteer to read the verses aloud. Ask:

- **What do these verses say about why we should forgive people who hurt us?**

Say: **Jesus said that if we want God to forgive us, we must forgive others. That sounds pretty harsh, as if Jesus meant business about this forgiveness stuff. Let's find out how we can become better forgivers when people hurt us.**

Real Forgiveness

(For this activity you will need pencils and a copy of the "Forgiving Friends" handout on page 41 for each student.)

Ask the students:

- **Why is it sometimes hard to forgive?**

After they have had an opportunity to respond, say: **One reason it is sometimes hard to forgive is because we have a misunderstanding about what forgiveness is.**

Distribute the "Forgiving Friends" handout. Point out the definition of what real forgiveness is and what forgiveness is not. Say: **Read each of the case studies on the handout. Then write down whether or not you think each story is an example of real forgiveness. Using the definition of forgiveness on the top of the handout, think about why you think this is or is not an example of forgiveness.**

After the students have completed their worksheets, allow them to explain whether they think each story is an example of forgiveness, and why.

Choose Your Closing

Option 1: Flushing Revenge

(For this activity you will need pens or markers, toilet paper, and a toilet.)

Give each person a pen or marker, and pass around a roll of toilet paper. Have students tear off one square for each friend that has recently hurt them. Have the students briefly write down on each square one way someone has hurt or wronged them. Have them also write down how they have tried or thought about getting revenge. Let the students know that they will not be asked to share what they write down. After the class members have completed this task, have them all take their toilet paper and throw it into the toilet. Flush the toilet. Close in prayer asking God to help you and your students to give up their plans for revenge and begin to forgive their friends.

Option 2: Weighed Down By Revenge

(For this activity you will need two weights, such as gallon milk jugs filled with water or sand. You will also need a stopwatch and a relay race course that has been marked off.)

Have students line up single file. Say: **We're going to have a cooperative race. Our goal is for everyone to take turns carrying these two milk jugs from this side of the room and back in the shortest time possible. When I start the timer, the first person will run as fast as he or she can to the other end of the room and then run all the way back here. When the runner gets back here, he or she will hand the two jugs to the next person in line, and so on. When the last person returns with the jugs, I will stop the timer. Our goal is to see how quickly we can do this as a group.**

When the group finishes the relay, say: **We are going to do the relay again, but this time we will first empty the two jugs. Let's see if in this race we can**

Leader Tip

If flushing the toilet paper is impractical for your group, then take your students outside and burn their toilet paper in a metal trash can.

finish the relay in less time.

When your group finishes the second relay, ask:

• **Which relay was easier? Why?**

• **Why was our time faster in the second race?**

Then say: **Sometimes if our unforgiving hearts are full of revenge, it makes us feel heavy inside. Our need to get back at those who hurt us keeps us from our goal of following Christ. In order to live like Christ, we need to drop our plans for revenge.**

Close in prayer, asking God to help your students forgive those who have hurt them.

Forgiving Friends

Read the following stories. Decide if you think each story is an example of real forgiveness. Using the definition of real forgiveness from this handout, tell why you think this is or is not real forgiveness.

Story 1

Two friends, Mike and Julio, are playing soccer. Mike makes fun of the way Julio is playing. When Julio tells Mike that he heard what Mike said, Mike apologizes for his remarks. Julio says he accept s Mike's apology. However, after school, Julio starts a rumor that the coach is thinking about kicking Mike off the team.

Is this real forgiveness? Why or why not?

Story 2

The last three times Mary borrowed one of Brian's CDs, she lost it. Each time Mary lost a CD, she said she was sorry. The fourth time she asked to use one of Brian's CDs, he told her, "I understand you are sorry for the loss of the other CDs, but you can't borrow any more until you help pay for some of the lost CDs."

Is this real forgiveness? Why or why not?

Story 3

Katherine forgot to invite Megan to her birthday party. This really hurt Megan's feelings. Later, Katherine realized her mistake. When Katherine started to apologize to Megan, Megan said, "My feelings weren't hurt. I didn't want to go to your party anyway."

Is this real forgiveness? Why or why not?

Story 4

Josh, the school bully, shoves Emily out of the lunch line at school. Emily tells Josh that she doesn't like to be pushed. Josh never says that he is sorry. At the end of math class, Emily offers to help Josh study for the upcoming math test.

Is this real forgiveness? Why or why not?

Reaching Hurting Friends

Friendship. Think about how that word impacts the kids in your group. They struggle to find the "right" friends. They struggle to keep those friendships. And they constantly struggle with what to do when their friends are hurting. Friendship is a complex web of trust, acceptance, and self-esteem for your kids. It's a delicate balance. And that balance is disturbed when their friends are hurting, broken, or stressed.

What do your kids do when their friends are hurting? Some of them run. Others try to help, but are unsure about what to do or how to do it. Still others just don't care. This lesson will help your kids understand the need to help their friends, and it'll give them some ideas how they can help their friends when they're hurting.

Choose Your Opening

Option 1: I've Been There

(For this activity you'll need index cards and pens.)

When kids have arrived, have them get in pairs. Say: **We've all had a friend who was experiencing something that was tough. And knowing what to do when our friends are going through hard times can be difficult. So let's talk about a time when our friends faced something tough, and what we might have done about it.**

Ask each student to share with his or her partner about a time when a friend faced something difficult. This might have been a serious illness or a death in the family, a divorce, a family member getting in trouble with the law, abuse at home, and so on. Instruct students to each write down the experience on the index card that you've given them. Tell them not to write out how they helped their friends, but just the difficulty their friends had.

When students are finished, ask pairs to trade index cards with another pair. Then tell your kids to write out what they'd do for their friends if they faced the situation on the cards they now hold. They should write their method of helping on the back of the card. When students are finished, have them return the index cards to the original owners, and read what the other students wrote. When kids are finished, ask volunteers to share their situations, what other students might do, and how they helped their friends. Then ask:

• What struggles do we face as we try to help hurting friends?

• Why can it be so difficult to reach out to hurting friends?

Say: **We've all got friends. And our friends are going to hurt now and then. God's Word gives us a great amount of information on how to reach out to hurting friends. Today we're going to discover what it says.**

Option 2: Unwrapping Friends

(For this activity you'll need four rolls of toilet paper, four packs of self-stick notes, and markers.)

Before kids arrive, place a roll of toilet paper, a pack of self-stick notes, and several markers in four separate locations around your meeting room.

As kids arrive, have them get in four separate groups. Say: **I'd like you to go to one of the activity centers I've set up, choose one person to wrap in toilet paper, and then use the entire roll of toilet paper to wrap up this person.**

Give kids time to wrap up their person. Then say: **Now I'd like you to imagine that this person is your very best friend, but he or she has a lot of problems. This person is really stressed out and doesn't know how to handle all of his or her problems. You've got to help this person identify all of the things that are problems. So take some time, write out some problems that someone your age might have, then stick them to the toilet paper.**

Give kids time to write out their ideas. When they're finished, have each group present its person and the problems he or she is having. Then say: **Great job! Now that you've identified your friend's problems, it's time for you to be a really good friend. You've got to help your friend get rid of all of his or her problems. Let's see how quickly you can do that. You've got five seconds to rip off the toilet paper and all the problems. I'm going to call time in exactly five seconds. Let's see how you do.**

Give students the signal to begin, then call time in exactly five seconds. Make sure that students stop when you call time. Then wander around the room and point out the problems that groups weren't able to help their friends get rid of.

Say: **Today we're going to talk about how we can help our friends when they're hurting. Helping hurting friends is like stripping problems off them. The Bible gives us some great ideas about how we can help our friends.**

The Bible Experience
An Example of Friendship

(For this activity you'll need one copy of the "Friendship Examination" handout from page 47 for each student. You'll also need Bibles and pencils.)

Say: **Sometimes it can be difficult to find a good example of what we should do to reach out to our hurting friends. I'd like you to look at the friendship of David and Jonathan, and learn how Jonathan helped David.**

Ask kids to stay in their four groups, or have them get into four groups if they aren't already. Assign each group one passage from the "Friendship Examination" handout. Instruct groups to read the passage and write out the answers that they find.

When students are finished, have them combine with another group to form two large groups. Instruct groups to share what they found in their passages. As groups are sharing, remind students to write down on their handouts the answers from the other group. When they're finished, have the original groups get together with a different group and repeat the process. Repeat one more time, until all groups have met together. When they're finished, have students form a circle in the center of the meeting room. Then ask:

• **What did you learn about friendship from reading and hearing about David and Jonathan's friendship?**

• **If you had been David, how would you have felt about what Jonathan did?**

• **Why was it important for Jonathan to help David?**

• **What the result of Jonathan's helping David?**

Say: **David and Jonathan had an amazing friendship. I'd like you to think about how Jonathan helped David. It's not always easy to reach out to hurting friends, but God wants us to do it.**

Reflection and Application
....

My Hurting Friends

(For this activity you'll need newsprint, tape, and a marker.)

Say: **Just like David and Jonathan, we've got friends who are hurting right now. Let's think about how we can apply what Jonathan did for David to our own lives.**

Have students get in pairs. Explain that you're going to read them a situation, and you'd like them to respond in two ways. First, you'd like them to think of the worst possible way to help this friend through the problem. Then you'd like them to think about how they could truly help this friend. Read aloud:

Jennifer has been your friend for years. She's gone with your family on vacation several times. She calls your mom, "Mom." She's as close to your family as she can be without actually being related. And all of that has been because her family isn't the greatest. Her parents divorced when she was young, and her mom has been struggling to pay the bills and raise the family at the same time. Recently, her mom has started dating a guy that's not the best influence on the family, and he's got a lot of tough friends, too. Lately, Jennifer has been coming to school really tired, and very angry. You finally got a chance to walk home with her yesterday, and you're seeing things that aren't usual for her. She's using a lot of bad words and she says that she's smoking. You want to help her. This isn't the Jennifer that you know. What can you do to help?

Give pairs time to think up positive and negative ways to help Jennifer. When they're ready, have students share their negative ways to help Jennifer. As they share, write their responses on the left side of a sheet of newsprint taped to the wall. When they're finished, draw a line down the center of the newsprint and ask groups to share the ways they could really help Jennifer. When you're finished, have students look at both columns of responses. Then ask:

- **What do you notice about helping friends from these two lists?**
- **What might happen to Jennifer if we choose not to help her?**
- **What might happen to Jennifer's life if we choose to help her?**
- **How might Jonathan have helped Jennifer?**

Say: **We have a choice. We can choose to help our friends, or we can choose to do nothing. When we choose to help, God can use us to change their lives. But choosing to help our friends doesn't always mean that we can solve their problems on our own. Choosing to help sometimes means getting somebody else involved, such as a parent, a teacher, or a counselor.**

Choose Your Closing

Option 1: Friendship Pictures

(For this activity you'll need a Bible, newsprint, and markers.)

Give each student a sheet of newsprint and several markers. Say: **I'd like you to think of a friend that's hurting right now. Then use the markers and newsprint I've given you to draw a picture of the two of you. Next, write some of the things you might say to your friend above your picture. Also write above your picture some things your friend might be thinking as you talk. Then, at the bottom of the picture, write out some of the things that might happen to your friend if you actually tried to help him or her.**

Give students time to draw their pictures. When they're finished, have students get in pairs and share their pictures if they are comfortable doing so. When pairs have shared, ask volunteers to share their pictures with the entire class. Do not force anyone to share who does not want to.

Say: **God's Word gives us a really great idea of what it means to be a friend. I'd like to read it to you.**

Read Ecclesiastes 4:9-12 aloud. Then say: **God wants us to be like this. He wants us to stand with our friends. When they're hurting, he wants us to help them. When we do that, our friends succeed, and we get to watch God working in their lives.**

Close the meeting with a short prayer. Encourage students to take their pictures with them as a reminder of the friends they want to help.

Option 2: My Hurting Friend

(For this activity you'll need a Bible, paper, and pencils.)

Say: **Just like David and Jonathan, we've got friends who are hurting right now. Even though we might not have all the answers, we should still try to help them. The Bible gives us some encouragement to help our friends.**

Read Ecclesiastes 4:9-12 aloud. Then ask:

- **What does the Bible say is the best way to help our friends?**
- **If we lived out what the Bible suggests, what might happen to our friendships?**

Instruct kids to think about a friend they have right now who is hurting. If students can't think of a hurting friend, ask them to think of one that they feel might need help with something. Give students a sheet of paper and a pencil. Ask students to write a letter to that friend, offering advice or comfort. When students are finished, have kids gather in the center of the meeting room. Ask volunteers to read their letters to the rest of the class.

Say: **God wants us to reach out to our hurting friends. He loves them, and he wants us to help them when they're hurting or scared.**

Ask students to hold their letters in front of them. Tell students that you're going to give them a few seconds to pray silently for the friends they wrote their letters to. When students are finished, pray aloud for them that they'll be able to reach out to their hurting friends.

Friendship Examination

1 Samuel 18:1-9

What David Did:

What Jonathan Did:

What Happened:

1 Samuel 19:1-11

What David Did:

What Jonathan Did:

What Happened:

1 Samuel 20:1-17

What David Did:

What Jonathan Did:

What Happened:

1 Samuel 20:18-42

What David Did:

What Jonathan Did:

What Happened:

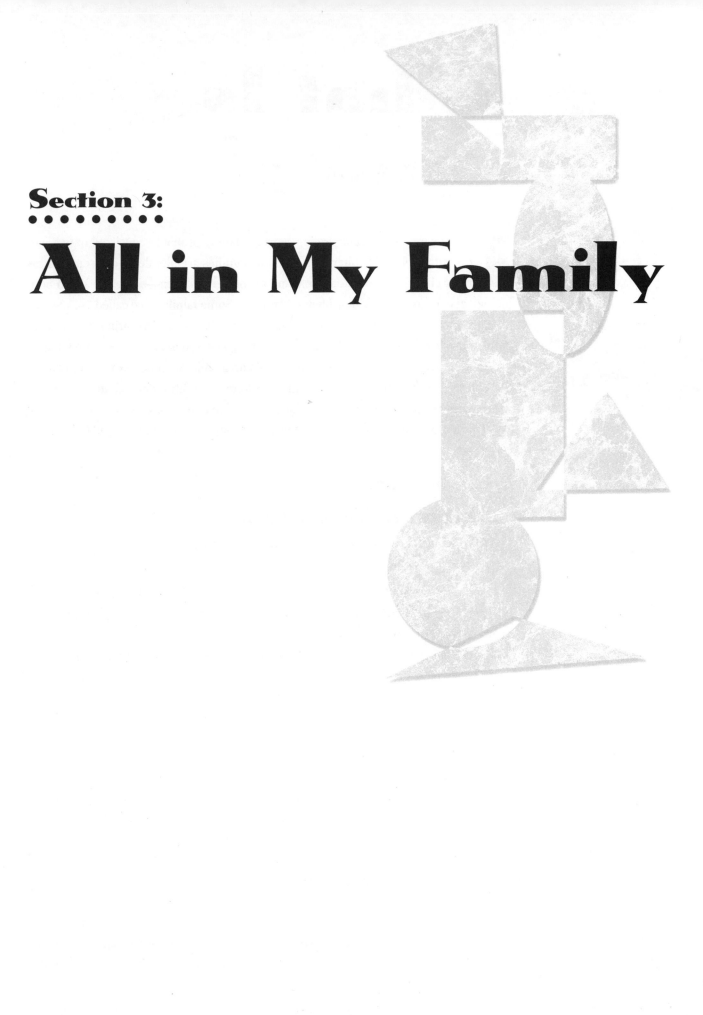

Section 3:
•••••••••
All in My Family

What Is Family?

In your parents' or grandparents' world, a family probably consisted of two parents with biological children. Now many families are blended—a parent and his or her children plus a stepparent and his or her children—sometimes with both biological parents forming new blended families. Some families are called "sandwich" families, meaning that parents are raising their children and also caring for an aging parent who lives with them. The media and the government are bringing new family groups to light, such as extended families raising a child or same-sex partners adopting children. Whether or not we would condone such situations, chances are that your youth either know a family like this or they are at least aware of them.

This lesson will help kids see that there are many types of families, and God values every person in them.

Choose Your Opening

Option 1: We Are Family

(For this activity you'll need a chalkboard and chalk; a white board and a marker; or newsprint, tape, and a marker.)

Begin this lesson by discussing what students' families are like. Ask the following questions, and as students offer their thoughts, write their answers on a white board, chalkboard, or newsprint taped to the wall.

Encourage students to honestly say what they feel, even if they don't think it's the "right" answer, such as, "I don't like that I have to share a room with my stepsister." You might also offer answers from your own family experience when you were a preteen to encourage kids to tell about their own experiences. Ask:

• **What do you like about your family?**
• **What do you not like about your family?**
• **Who makes up your family?**
• **Do you consider any people who are not blood relatives to be part of your family?**

Say: **There are several different kinds of families represented here in our class. But I bet there are even more types of families in the world. Let's brainstorm different types of families. What kinds of groups of people can make up a family?**

If students don't offer these answers, add the following families to the list: single parent families, blended families, families with only one child, families with lots of children, children raised by grandparents or other family members, singles, couples without children, families with adopted children, and empty nesters (older couples whose children are grown).

Say: **God knows that there are all these different kinds of families in the world, and he loves all of them.**

Option 2: My Family Tree

(For this activity you'll need pictures or drawings of different kinds of trees. You can cut them out of magazines, bring in an encyclopedia, or take pictures of trees around your neighborhood. Make sure you include a picture of a tree that splits off into more than one major branch, or one that appears to have more than one trunk. You'll also need a copy of a family tree from a Bible or some other source, or you may sketch your own family tree.)

Say: **Let's look at these pictures. They all show trees, but the trees are different from each other.**

Ask:

• **How are they similar and different?** Students might say that the leaves or bark differ from one tree to another. Trees may also differ or appear similar in size, shape, and coloring.

Say: **When people talk about the generations of their family, they sometimes use what's called a family tree to keep track of the people they're related to and what the relationships are between everyone.** Hold up the example of a family tree. **This is what a family tree looks like.** (Or "This is my family tree" if you're using an example of your own.)

Let's look at these tree pictures again. Each kind of tree has a different shape and personality to its appearance.

Ask:

• **Which tree reminds you of your family? Why?**

Allow kids to take turns calling out their choices and ask them to briefly explain why they chose a particular tree.

The Bible Experience
....
God's Family

(For this activity you'll need at least one Bible for each group, a copy of the "Families in the Bible" handout on page 54 for each group, and pencils.)

Say: **In the New Testament, the term *family* generally referred to a husband and wife and their children. But during some times in history, including Old Testament times, *family* meant extended family, including all the aunts, uncles, cousins, grandparents, and in-laws you could find. But people also considered friends, servants, boarders, and guests to be part of the family too. So while we usually think of family as being blood relatives, family can include other people that you think of as family even if they're not technically related to you.**

There are many families in the Bible; let's look at just a few of them today.

Divide your class into five groups and assign each group one of the following Bible passages to look up and read together. If you have a large class, you may assign one passage to more than one group.

- Genesis 4:1-10
- Genesis 25:24-27; 27:41
- Ruth 1:1-18
- Esther 2:7-9, 20
- Luke 2:41-49

Ask students to discuss the questions on the handout and write down brief answers. Have each group also choose a spokesperson to report to the class about their passage.

When groups have had time to read and come up with answers, bring everyone together again and ask the spokespeople to share their answers with the rest of the class.

Say: **These are just a few examples of families in the Bible. And as we've seen, biblical families were made up of many different kinds of relationships. We've also seen that some families got along well, while others had intense clashes between family members. Some even wanted to kill each other! Now let's take a look at what our family relationships are supposed to be like.**

Ask for four volunteers to read the following Scripture verses aloud: Luke 18:29-30, Ephesians 6:1-4, and 1 Timothy 5:4.

Say: **We've all had times when we didn't get along with a family member. You've probably had fights with a brother or sister, and you've disobeyed your parents at least once.**

Ask:

- **What do these verses say about how we should treat members of our family?**
- **What do the verses in Luke tell us about priorities in our lives?**

Say: **We've seen that God wants us to honor our family members, to treat them with love and respect. And when it comes to our parents, we are to obey them. God's Word also tells us that our families should be such a high priority in our lives that only spreading God's kingdom should come before them. Let's see how we can be better contributing members in our families.**

Reflection and Application

Making Family Memories

(For this activity you'll need enough strips of colored paper, approximately 1½x6 inches, for each student to have several, plus a resealable plastic bag and marker or pen for each student.)

During this time you will guide students in making family memory jars. Have preteens write down a family memory on each strip of paper. Memories can be funny, happy, touching, or anything about their families that is meaningful to them such as a family vacation, a special holiday moment, a loving action done by a sibling, or a memory of a deceased relative. After writing each memory, instruct students to fold the slip of paper in half. Spend about ten minutes recording memories on paper strips.

Have each student collect his or her memory strips and seal them in the plastic bags so they don't get lost on the way home. Also give students plenty of blank slips of paper to take home with them. Encourage them to add more of their memories to the collection when they get home.

Tell students to give each of their family members strips of paper to record memories. Tell them to collect the memories from all of their family members in a jar or some other container with a lid. Then encourage them to help their parents plan a family night when everyone in the family takes turns drawing slips out of the jar and reading them aloud.

Choose Your Closing

Option 1: All My Brothers, Sisters, and Me

End this lesson with a time of prayer. Lead students in thanking God for family members. Name family members, such as moms, dads, siblings, grandparents, and other family members, then allow time for students to pray aloud or silently for those people in their lives. Close the prayer time by asking God to help each member of the families represented in your class to treat the others how God would want them to.

Another option, instead of saying full prayers as you name each type of family member, would be for students to simply say a word or phrase that summarizes what they want to thank God for about that person. For example, when you say "dad," students could pray "teacher," "friend," or "provider."

Option 2: Family Ring

(For this activity you'll need one 1x10-inch strip of construction paper and several 1x6-inch strips of construction paper for each student; markers; and glue, tape, or staplers.)

Have kids each write "God" on the 1x10-inch strip of construction paper, and then glue, tape, or staple the two ends together, forming a circle. Then have them select a strip of paper for each member of their family they live with, including themselves. Instruct them to write each person's name on a separate strip. Then have them wrap each strip around the God strip and connect the ends together, forming circles so that each person's name loop is connected to the God loop. The result should be like a key ring—the God loop is the key ring, and the family names are like keys attached to the ring.

Once everyone has a family ring, say: **Remember that God made families, he values all kinds of families, and he is the one who helps families stick together. Let's thank God for our families.**

Close with prayer.

Families in the Bible

- Which Scripture passage are you studying?

- How are the family members in this passage related?

- What situation are the family members dealing with?

- What kind of relationship do they have?

- How might the situation in this family be similar to something your family has experienced?

Sibling Rivalry

Getting along with siblings is sometimes very difficult for preteens. Emotions run high at this age, and conflict is common. However, there are some practical things preteens can do to improve their relationships with their siblings.

This lesson will give kids some insight as to when and where their sibling conflict occurs and some practical advice on how to avoid arguments.

Choose Your Opening

Option 1: Draw Your House

(For this activity you will need paper and a pencil for each student.)

Preteens typically are not aware of their behavior. This exercise is designed to help them see when and where their conflict with brothers and sisters typically takes place.

Give each student paper and a pencil. Say: **I would like you to draw the floor plan of where you live. Draw the location of each room in your house or apartment. Keep your drawing simple. Label each room, such as "bathroom," "kitchen," or "my sister's room."** It might be helpful if you show your students an example of the floor plan of your own home.

When they have completed their drawings, have the students form groups of three. Say: **In your groups, show the drawings of your homes. As you show your drawing, tell your group where each member of your family spends most of his or her time at home.**

When students have finished sharing, say: **Now share with your group in which two rooms you and your sisters or brothers have the most arguments and fights.**

Ask:

• **What do you fight about in those two rooms?**

After they have all shared, tell your students to hang on to their drawings to use again later. Say: **All of us have had some conflict with our siblings. Today we are going to explore ways that we can improve our relationships with our brothers and sisters.**

Option 2: Tied Together

(For this activity you will need a two-foot section of rope for each pair of students.)

Randomly pair off students. Draw their names out of a hat, or give each student a numbered slip of paper. It doesn't matter how you pair them off, as long as it's random and they have no choice on who is their partner. When they have been placed in pairs, instruct them to tie the right ankle of one partner to the left ankle of the second partner. After they have done this, give the entire class several tasks they must perform while tied to their partners. For example, have them walk around the church, climb over a series of chairs, or play tag.

When all the tasks have been completed and you have untied your kids, ask:

- **Which tasks were the hardest for you and your partner? Why?**
- **How did your partner help you carry out your tasks?**
- **What are some of the things you and your partner had to do in order to complete the tasks?**

Say: **In this activity you were tied to someone you did not choose. It's the same in your family life: You did not get to choose your brothers or sisters, but now you are bound with them in a family. Today we're going to look at how we can be successful in the task of getting along with our siblings.**

The Bible Experience

Family Counseling

(For this activity you will need a Bible for each student and one sheet of paper and a pencil for each group.)

Form groups of two or three. You may use the same groups you used in the opening activity if you like. Give each group a sheet of paper and a pencil. Make sure each student has a Bible. Read aloud Genesis 37:2-11 to your students as they follow along in their Bibles.

After reading this passage, say: **In this story we meet a family that definitely has some problems, especially between Joseph and his brothers. Pretend that you are a family counselor. Jacob, Joseph, and his brothers have come to you for family counseling. In your groups, brainstorm what advice you might give to Jacob, the father; Joseph, the younger brother; and Joseph's ten older brothers.**

Ask:

- **What would you tell each of them to do in order to help the family?**

Have one person in each group record what advice the group would give each family member. When they have finished, have the group's recorder share their advice with the whole class.

Say: **Besides just making things more pleasant and livable, and not killing each other, why is it so important for brothers and sisters to get along? Let's find out what the Bible has to say.**

Have your students turn in their Bibles to 1 John 2. Ask a volunteer to read aloud verses 9-11. Then ask another volunteer to read aloud 1 John 4:19-21. Ask:

- **What does the way we treat our brothers and sisters say about our love for God?**

Say: **John makes it pretty clear here that if we don't love others, then we don't love God either, and if we say that we do, we are liars. If we want to show God and others how much we love him, then we better start at home by showing how much we love our brothers and sisters. Let's look at some ways we can do that.**

Can't We All Just Get Along?

(For this activity you will need a white board or a piece of poster board and a marker.)

Have the following written on the white board or poster board:

Helpful advice for getting along with your brothers and sisters:

- Ask before borrowing his or her stuff.
- Don't barge into his or her room uninvited.
- Apologize when you are wrong.
- Refuse to get into dumb arguments.
- Say only what is helpful or encouraging.
- Treat your sibling the way you would like to be treated.

Break up the class into six groups. Assign each group one of the advice statements above. Tell them: **I want your group to think of a situation in which your helpful advice would be useful. You are going to make up a quick skit in which the brothers and sisters either forget to follow the advice or remember to use it. You may use props if you want, but remember that the whole skit should last only a minute or two. Make it very obvious which piece of advice you are demonstrating so that the rest of the class can easily guess.**

After students have performed their skits, have them remain in their skit groups. Ask the following questions, one at a time, allowing a few minutes between questions for youth to share their answers with the other members of their group. Ask:

- **Which one of these pieces of advice do you already follow with your brother or sister?**
- **In which area do you need to improve?**
- **What else could you do to get along better with your brother or sister?**
- **If you started to try to improve your relationship with your siblings, how do you think they would respond?**

Option 1: Return of Draw Your House

(Use this option if you used Choose Your Opening Option 1. You will need the house drawings that your students created in that activity.)

Have the students return to their share groups formed during Choose Your Opening Option 1. Say: **Pick one room from your house drawing in which you have the most conflict with one of your siblings. Tell your group one specific and practical thing you can do to improve your relationship with your brother or sister in that room.**

End your time together by praying for your students as they try to improve their relationships with their brothers and sisters.

Leader Tip

If your class is small, divide into two or three groups, and assign each group to come up with skits for two or three of the pieces of advice.

Option 2: My Brother, My Friend

(For this activity you will need a white board and marker or a chalkboard and chalk.)

Have your students brainstorm on the topic: "How I would want to be treated by a friend." Write their answers on your white board. Then have them brainstorm on the topic: "How I would *not* like to be treated by a friend." Again, write their responses on the board.

Say: **Sometimes we think of our siblings as enemies. It's me against them. But imagine what it would be like if your brother or sister were one of your closest friends. You can't make them treat you like a friend, but you can choose to start treating them like a friend. Look at what we wrote on the board and choose one way you're going be a friend to your sibling.**

Close your time together by having your students silently pray for their siblings and for their relationships with their siblings. Close the prayer time yourself.

Family Struggles

Goal:
To support your family members.

Scripture Verses:
Exodus 20:12; Romans 13:1; Ephesians 6:1-4

Although many preteens are still eager to please their parents, they are also beginning to want more independence from them. They are beginning to look to peers for advice and acceptance more than to their parents. But this growing independence does not need to blossom into rebellion; healthy family relationships are possible, especially with God at the core.

In this lesson your students will learn the wisdom of treating their parents with honor, respect, and obedience.

Choose Your Opening

Option 1: Dear Blabby

(For this activity you will need pencils and paper, plus a basket or box.)

Say: **Does anybody know what an advice column in the newspaper is— such as "Ann Landers" or "Dear Abby"? Today, we're going to give you an opportunity to not only write asking for advice, but also to play the part of Ann Landers or Dear Abby. Our topic is family struggles. That's actually a pretty typical topic for these kinds of columns.**

First of all, I want each of you to write a letter to Dear Blabby about a struggle your family may have. Often, people sign their letters with made-up names. You may sign your real name or make up a name, but please try to write the letter about a real struggle in your family. You have five minutes to write your letters.

After kids have completed their letters, collect them in some kind of basket or box. Let kids take turns coming up in order of their birthdays, starting in November. Have kids each draw one letter, read it aloud, and offer advice for the family situation. If anyone chooses his or her own letter, have the student put it back and choose again.

When all the letters have been read and commented on, say: **Today we're going to find out what kind of advice God gives us in the Bible for getting along with our families.**

Option 2: What Irks Your Parents?

(For this activity, you will need a white board and marker.)

Open your class session by asking students:

• **Are there some things that you do or don't do that irk your parents?**

Say: **Let's think about what these are, and we'll make a list on the board.**

Record students' ideas on the board as they share. Then ask:

• **What are some specific things that your parents do or don't do that irritate you?**

Repeat the sharing time, and make a list on the board. Leave these on the board for a later activity. Say: **Today we are going to find out what the Bible says about parents and children, and how we can all get along better.**

The Bible Experience
A Command With a Promise

(For this activity you will need Bibles, a white board, and a marker.)

Say: **Open your Bibles to Romans 13:1.**

Have a volunteer read the verse aloud. Ask:

• **Who are some of the people who have authority over you?** Write the students' answers on the board. These may include teachers, coaches, and police. If nobody mentions parents, mention it yourself and add it to the list.

• **Why do you think God put parents in authority over children?** Students may suggest things such as to keep children safe, to teach children, and to provide for children.

Say: **Let's look at a Scripture passage in the Old Testament. Please turn to Exodus 20:12.**

Have a volunteer read this verse aloud. Ask:

• **How does this verse say that children should treat their parents?**

Say: **Now let's look at the same idea in the New Testament and see how it compares. Turn in your Bibles to Ephesians 6:1-4.**

Read these verses aloud while students follow along. Ask:

• **How is this passage different from the Old Testament passage?** The New Testament passage refers to the Old Testament by pointing out that this is the first commandment with a promise. Make sure kids get this idea, and that they know what the promise is. The New Testament also adds the admonition to parents.

Ask:

• **These verses use two different words to tell children how to relate to their parents. What are they?** ("Obey" and "honor.")

• **What's the difference between obeying and honoring?** Obedience means following our parents' will for us, doing what they tell us to do. To honor our parents means to respect them, not talk back, and obey them cheerfully.

• **Why do you think God wants us to obey and honor our parents?** Our parents deserve our obedience and honor because God put them in authority over us. Also, obedience and honor will make our parents' difficult job of raising us much easier.

Say: **Let's read the promise again.**

Have a volunteer read aloud verse 3. Ask:

• **What very practical things can you think of that illustrate the truth of this promise?**

• **How could obeying your parents give you a long life?**

• **How could disobeying your parents shorten your life?** Students might say that parents know best about their children's safety. A child who does not obey his parents but plays in the street might get hit by a car and killed. A child who experiments with smoking, drugs, or alcohol, even though her parents tell her not to, will probably not live as long as somebody that does not experiment with those things. Other examples could include guns, premarital sex, and gang involvement.

Say: **Usually, most parents want the best for their children and will try to make their lives healthy and safe. So obeying your parents can have a very practical payoff.**

Reflection and Application

Role-Play

(For this activity you'll need a white board and markers.)

Say: **Now we're going to do some role-plays to see if we can apply what the Bible says to some everyday family situations. All families have struggles from time to time. What things does your family struggle with?** Make a list on the white board as students share. If you used the Choose Your Opening Option 2, refer again now to the list you have already created.

Say: **I need some volunteers for a role-play.** Recruit volunteers based on the needs of each situation. For example, if the struggle is with a child keeping his or her room clean, you will need volunteers to play the roles of one or both parents, plus the preteen. In order to help kids understand, you might want to take part in the first role-play. When your role-play reaches a point of serious conflict, step out and ask a student volunteer to take your place. The students should work together to offer suggestions for solutions to the conflict. Remind class members that the Bible gives us both a command and a promise for obeying and honoring our parents—"that it may go well with you and that you may enjoy long life on the earth" (Ephesians 6:3).

As long as the role-plays are working, do as many of the real situations that your kids have suggested as you time for.

Choose Your Closing

Option 1: Letter to Parents

(For this activity you will need paper, pencils, envelopes, and copies of the "Letter to Parents" handout from page 63.)

Say: **We're going to have an opportunity now to write a letter to our parents that will include the things that we've discussed today.**

Distribute the "Letter to Parents" handout.

Say: **This is a fill-in form letter. I'd like you to fill in the blanks to write a real letter that you will take home and share with your parents. If you have additional things you want to say, put them at the bottom as a P.S. If there are choices in parentheses, cross out the ones that don't apply and circle the ones that do.**

Give students a few minutes to work. Then say: **Now I'd like for you to write**

one more letter. This one is also to your parents, but it will be about "What I wish my parents knew about me, and how I wish they would treat me."

Distribute paper and give students about five minutes to complete their letters. Then have them seal their letters in envelopes and address them to their parents. Encourage your students to either hand-deliver the letters to their parents, or offer to put them in the mail yourself. Collect any letters that students want you to mail, and be sure to add correct postage and mail them within the next couple of days. Let your students choose to send either one or both of their letters, or neither one.

Close class in prayer, thanking God for families and asking him to continue to be a part of your students' families as they strive for better relationships.

Option 2: Family Game Night

(For this activity you will need paper, pencils, and a white board and marker.)

Say: **Families that spend time together usually grow closer.**
Ask:

• **What are some fun things that your family could do to spend more time together?**

Write students' suggestions on the board. Make sure family game night gets on the list, even if you have to suggest it yourself. Ask:

• **What are some things that you would need to think about if you decided to get a family game night going at your house?** Write students' ideas on the board, and encourage kids to write down the ideas as well so that they can use them at home. Your ideas should include the following:

- How to present the idea to the family.
- How to interest parents and siblings of all ages.
- A process for choosing games.
- Refreshments.
- Who should organize the game night.
- What day and time.
- How often.

Close class in prayer, thanking God for families and asking him to continue to be a part of your students' families as they strive for better relationships.

Letter to Parents

Fill in the blanks or cross out words in parentheses that don't apply.

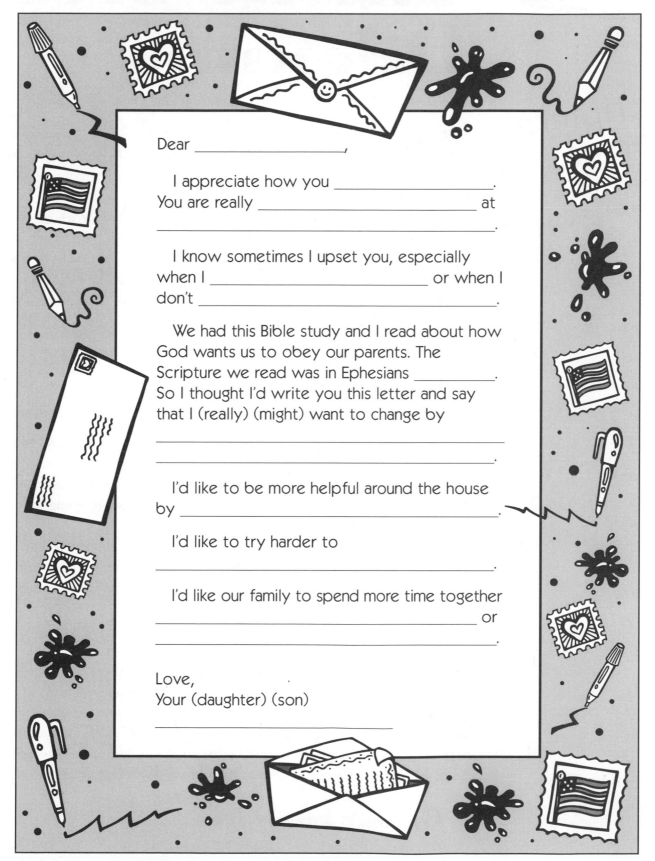

Dear _____,

I appreciate how you _____.
You are really _____ at
_____.

I know sometimes I upset you, especially
when I _____ or when I
don't _____.

We had this Bible study and I read about how
God wants us to obey our parents. The
Scripture we read was in Ephesians _____.
So I thought I'd write you this letter and say
that I (really) (might) want to change by

_____
_____.

I'd like to be more helpful around the house
by _____.

I'd like to try harder to
_____.

I'd like our family to spend more time together
_____ or
_____.

Love,
Your (daughter) (son)

_____

The Divorce Dilemma

Divorce has touched every student in your class. Many of the preteens in your group have seen their lives ripped apart as their parents parted ways. Some experience a less-direct connection, having seen divorce through lost aunts or uncles, or a friend who is now gone every weekend.

Preteens experience intense emotion when it comes to divorce. They have difficulty expressing these emotions, and an even more difficult time identifying the source of their behavior and feelings. Unfortunately, much of the healing comes only with time and maturity. You can help the kids in your group start the healing process on the right foundation. You can help them see that they are not to blame and that God loves them, their mothers, and their fathers as much as he has ever loved them.

Choose Your Opening

Option 1: Torn in Two

(For this activity you will need clear tape and magazine pictures of families.)

Say: **Today we're going to talk about a difficult subject: divorce. Some of your parents may be divorced. Some of your friends' parents may be divorced. No matter what your experience is with divorce, I want you to know that God cares about you and your family. To begin, we're going to look at some of the feelings that surround divorce.**

Give each person a picture of a family from a magazine. Have preteens rip their pictures into small pieces. Then have each person work to put his or her picture back together using the tape. After kids have succeeded or given up, form pairs, and have preteens discuss:

- **How is what you did to the pictures like divorce? How is it different?**
- **What are some of the feelings that surround divorce?**
- **How can we help friends if their parents get divorced?**

Say: **Divorce is painful. But believe it or not, God can and will heal our hurts. Let's look into this some more. But first, let's pray.** Pray whatever prayer is appropriate for the reactions and responses you've observed. For example, if students were very solemn during the activity, pray that God would heal and help them. If preteens were jovial, pray that God will help them understand how divorce affects people's lives.

Option 2: Family Tree

(For this activity you'll need a pencil and a copy of the "Family Tree" handout from page 68 for each student.)

Distribute pencils and "Family Tree" handouts to preteens. Say: **Today we're going to talk about divorce. It's a difficult subject because many people have experienced a lot of pain through the divorce of loved ones. We're going to start to see how divorce may affect your family. I'd like you to fill out this family tree. Start with your name and your brothers' and sisters' names at the bottom. Put your parents' names above yours. Put your uncles' and aunts' names beside your parents' names, and your grandparents' names above your parents' names. As you fill out your family tree, try to include all of your stepparents, stepbrothers, stepsisters, and step-grandparents too. If anyone in your family has been divorced, put a D by his or her name.**

Help kids work on their handouts. When they finish, ask:

• **How many of you don't have any D's on your handout?**

• **As you look at your sheet, how do you think divorce has affected people in your family?**

• **Why do you think divorce is such a painful thing?**

Say: **Believe it or not, God can heal the hurts caused by divorce. Let's look into this some more.**

The Bible Experience

Everlasting Love

(For this activity you will need thread, yarn, twine, and rope, each cut into lengths of approximately eighteen inches, enough for half your students. You'll also need Bibles, newsprint, tape, and a marker.)

Have preteens form pairs. Give each pair a length of thread, yarn, twine, and rope. Say: **Have each person in your pair take one end of the thread. When I say "go," try to break apart the thread. Go!**

Continue this process with each of the materials you've brought. Then have pairs discuss the following questions. You might want to write them on the board or on a sheet of newsprint where everyone can see. Otherwise, allow students a few minutes to discuss each question with their partners before you move on to ask the next one. Ask:

• **Why were you able to break some of these strings but not others?**

• **Read Romans 8:35-39. Which of the materials you tried to break is most like God's love for you and your families? Explain.**

• **Does God love people who go through a divorce? Does God love their children? How do you know?**

• **What's the most painful thing you've ever gone through?**

• **How did God help you through that time?**

Ask volunteers to share with the class what they discussed. Then read aloud Romans 8:35-39. Say: **God cares about you and your family. There is nothing that can separate you from God's love—no matter how bad or difficult the situation might be. And God promises to be with us through all our struggles, even divorce.**

Have students turn in their Bibles to Psalm 2:7, and ask a volunteer to read this verse aloud. Ask:

• **How can this verse be comforting to someone whose parents are going through a divorce?**

Have students turn to Psalm 68:4-6, and ask a volunteer to read these verses aloud. Ask:

• **How do these verses make you feel?**

Finally, have students turn to Romans 8:15-16, and ask a volunteer to read these verses aloud. Ask:

• **What do these verses tell us?**

• **How does it make you feel to know that God is your father and you are his child?**

Say: **No matter what our earthly families look like or are going through, everyone who believes in Jesus is part of an even bigger, perfect family. God will take care of us. Even when people are going through a divorce, God still loves everyone involved! He hurts for them and with them, but he still loves them all and cares for them.**

Reflection and Application

If I Could Tell You

(For this activity you'll need a Bible, and paper, a pencil, and an envelope for each student.)

Say: **I'd like for us to take some time to deal with some of the feelings that go along with divorce. I'd like for each of you to write a letter to God, to your mom or dad, or to another person involved in a divorce that has affected you or someone in your family. You don't necessarily have to send the letter—this is more about how you and God feel about the situation. Try to work part or all of the passage we read from Romans 8:35-39 into your letter. If divorce hasn't affected you in any way, write the letter to God about a friend you know who has been affected by divorce, or write your letter to that friend.**

Give each student a sheet of paper, a pencil, and an envelope, and give them plenty of time to write. When preteens finish, give them an opportunity to share their letters or thoughts and feelings concerning divorce. Make certain to have the group pray for students who show strong emotion. Offer to help kids who want assistance in delivering their letters.

Choose Your Closing

Option 1: It's Not Your Fault

(For this activity blow up and tie off two balloons for each student. You'll also need masking tape.)

Use masking tape to mark off a square in the middle of your room that's big enough to hold all the balloons you prepared. Designate one-third of your students to be the Returners. The remaining students will be the Removers.

Say: **Returners, it's your job to make sure all of the balloons stay inside the masking-tape box I've created. Removers, it's your job to make sure the** balloons stay out of the box. Both Returners and Removers may only use their feet to move the balloons. Are there any questions about this game?

Answer questions, then begin the game. After a few minutes of play, stop the game and discuss these questions with your class members:

• **What was it like to be a Remover? a Returner?**

• **Do you think the Returners could have kept all of the balloons in the square if they just would have tried harder? Why or why not?**

• **Can children keep their parents from divorcing if they try hard enough?**

• **What can and can't children do if their parents get a divorce?**

Say: **No matter how hard the Returners tried, they couldn't keep all of the balloons in the square—it was simply beyond their control. A child can pray for his or her parents if they're going through a divorce. But no matter how much or how hard the child prays, the parents still have to make a decision. If your parents are divorced, I want you to know that it's not your fault. Nothing you could have done would have made a difference. It was simply beyond your control.**

Close class in prayer, thanking God that he loves us and is always with us. Ask for him to comfort all those who are hurting because of divorce.

Option 2: Reminder Bracelets

(For this activity you'll need gold beads, beads of various colors, scissors, and narrow leather strands.)

Say: **God cares about you and God cares about your family. We're going to make reminders that no matter how difficult things are in our lives, God is with us and will help us.**

Have each student cut a length of the leather strip long enough to tie around his or her wrist or ankle. Give each preteen two gold beads and say: **The first gold bead represents God, and the second gold bead represents you, because you're God's child. Thread your leather strip through the two beads. Now I'd like for you to surround the two gold beads with beads that represent troubles and sorrows in your life. For example, if your parents' divorce makes you very sad, you can put blue beads on the outside of the gold beads. If you're angry about something that has happened to you, put a red bead on each side of the gold ones. Put about six beads on your string in addition to the gold ones.**

When students are done threading their leather strips, have them help each other tie the leather and beads around their wrists or ankles. Encourage students to tie the bracelets on their backpacks if they'd rather not wear them.

Say: **No matter what comes against you, God is with you. He cares for you and your family even in the most difficult times. When you feel alone or hurt, remember the two gold beads that remind us that God is always with us. Even after these bracelets get old and break, or you cut them off, God is still with you.**

Close class in prayer, thanking God that he loves us and is always with us. Ask for him to comfort all those who are hurting because of divorce.

Family Tree

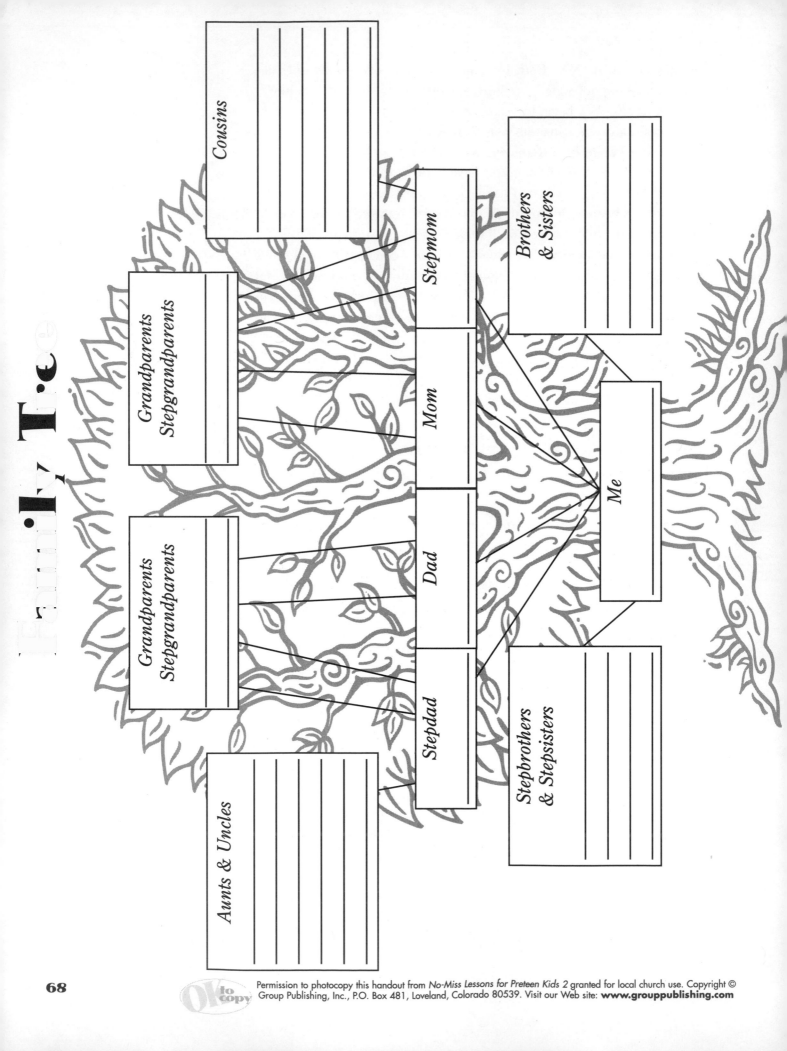

Cousins

Grandparents
Stepgrandparents

Grandparents
Stepgrandparents

Aunts & Uncles

Stepmom

Mom

Dad

Stepdad

Brothers
& Sisters

Me

Stepbrothers
& Stepsisters

Section 4:

My Constantly Changing World

Goal:
....
To use the Internet wisely.

E-Smarts

Scripture Verses:
Proverbs 4:23-27; John 14:6; Philippians 4:8-9; Colossians 3:5-6, 17; 1 Timothy 5:13; 6:10-12; James 1:13-15; 1 Peter 1:13-15; 1 John 1:9; 4:19-21

Many preteens have already experienced or have at least heard of most on-line dangers. They already have or soon will have access and the knowledge to find damaging material. The church must prepare preteens for the dangers and opportunities in the age of the Internet. It is our hope that this study helps you begin to prepare preteens to make wise choices in their world.

Choose Your Opening

Option 1: Good or Evil

(For this activity you'll need sheets of newsprint and markers.)

Have preteens form groups of four. Give each group a sheet of newsprint and a marker. Say: **There are many things in this world that can be used to glorify God or to work for evil. For example, a hammer can be used to build a home, or it can be used as a weapon. Draw a line down the middle of your newsprint. On the left side write "Evil." On the right side, write "Good." I'm going to assign each group at least one thing that can be used for good or evil. With your group, list all of the ways it can be used for good and all of the ways it can be used for evil.**

Give each group at least one of the following items to think about. Make sure you assign "the Internet" to at least one group.

- money
- television
- music
- time
- the Internet
- power
- authority

Leader Tip

Warning: In an effort to help preteens avoid the very real dangers of the Internet, this study covers material that some may find objectionable. Please prayerfully preview this lesson before planning to use it with preteens. You may want to consider inviting parents to the meeting or explaining to parents beforehand what you plan to cover with their children.

Give preteens about five minutes to work. Then have each group share its list, saving the Internet group for last. Ask:

- **What surprised you about the lists you made?**
- **Are the things we evaluated evil or good in themselves?**
- **Why do people sometimes choose to use these things for evil?**

Leader Tip

If your class is small, assign more than one thing for each group to consider.

Say: **God has given us many wonderful things, and he's given us the wisdom to create some amazing things. It seems as if we have choices with everything we encounter. We can either use things to build others up and glorify God, or we can use things for evil and to tear others down. The Internet is especially amazing. It's completely changing the way the world works and communicates. There are many wonderful things that can be done on the Internet. However there are a lot of dangers, too. Let's take some time to look at how we can use the Internet wisely.**

Option 2: Chat

(For this activity you'll need newsprint, tape, and markers.)

Tape one sheet of newsprint to the wall for every four students in your class, and place at least one marker near each sheet. Have your class members form groups of four and sit on the floor near one of the sheets taped to the walls. In their groups, have students number off from one to four.

Say: **How many of you have been in a chat room on the Internet? We're going to have our own chat right now. I'd like everyone to turn his or her back to the sheet of paper. When I call your number, I'd like you to go to your sheet of paper and write down a message. You can begin by just saying "hello," you can ask a question, or you can suggest a topic for the chat room such as sports or music. When I call another number, the person who is writing should sit down and face away from the sheet of paper while the next person comes up to chat. Are there any questions?**

Allow kids to "chat" for about five minutes by calling out numbers from one to four. When the chat is over, ask:

- **How was this like a real chat on the Internet?**
- **How was it different?**
- **What do you like about Internet chats? What do you dislike?**

Say: **Chatting on the Internet can be fun. You can talk to people from all over the country or people who live on the other side of the world. But you also need to know that there are some dangers that come with chatting on the Internet. Unfortunately, some people use the Internet—including chat rooms—to find the next victims of their crimes. Even though you think you're sure that you're talking to a harmless kid from far away, you could be talking to a clever man or woman in your town who wants to get enough information to cause you harm. We don't need to be frightened when we're on the Internet, but we do need to be careful. It's really important not to give out personal information online, such as your address, telephone number, or last name, unless your parents are absolutely certain it's OK.**

Ask:

- **Do you think it's important to be careful while you're online? Why or why not?**
- **How can the Internet be used for fun and good?**
- **How can the Internet be used for evil things?**

If you feel your students can handle a discussion on Internet-based crime, consider talking to them about how the Internet has been used to cheat people out of money, steal a person's identity, find victims for molestation, exploit children, sabotage computers, and other crimes. Make sure parents are notified if you plan on tackling some of the more graphic issues.

The Bible Experience

Surf City

(For this activity you will need Bibles, paper, pencils, newsprint, tape, and a marker.)

Tape a large sheet of newsprint to the wall.

Have kids form groups of three. Give each group a sheet of paper and a pencil. Say: **The Bible doesn't mention the Internet or computers. But the Bible gives us some very specific guidelines that apply to using the Internet. I'm going to assign a passage to each group. Look up your passage, then work with your group to come up with a summary of what the passage says.**

Assign one of the following passages to each group. If you have more than thirty kids, assign the same passage to more than one group. If you have fewer than thirty kids, assign more than one passage to each group as necessary, or choose only the most appropriate and relevant passages.

- Colossians 3:17
- Philippians 4:8-9
- Proverbs 4:23-27
- 1 Peter 1:13-15
- James 1:13-15
- 1 Timothy 5:13
- 1 Timothy 6:10-12
- Colossians 3:5-6
- 1 John 4:19-21
- John 14:6

After a few minutes, have each group read aloud its passage and its summary of the passage. Write the reference and the summary on the sheet of butcher paper. When everyone has shared, ask for a couple of volunteers to sum up the main idea of all these passages. Ask your kids to remain in their groups for the next activity.

Reflection and Application

Don't Go There

(For this activity you'll need paper, pencils, and copies of the "Don't Go There!" handout on page 75, cut apart.)

Before the lesson, make one photocopy of the "Don't Go There!" handout for every eighteen kids in your class and cut apart the strips on the handout. If you have fewer than eighteen kids, simply use fewer Web site descriptions, or have each group cover more than one.

Say: **We've covered just a few of the passages in the Bible that give us some guidelines when it comes to using the Internet. I'm going to give each group a description of a Web site. With your group, I'd like you to list all of the reasons a person should go to that site and all the reasons a person should *not* go to that site. Please use the Bible summaries we've listed as much as possible.**

Leader Tip

Warning: We have put extra characters in these fictitious Web sites that will produce error messages. However, if kids remove the extra characters and look up the Web sites, they may find objectionable material on the Web. You might want to collect the handouts after class just in case.

Give each group one or more of the sections from the "Don't Go There!" hand-out, paper, and pencils. Monitor groups closely as they work, and help them come up with reasons to avoid the Web sites they're investigating.

Have each group share its list, making sure to elaborate on reasons to avoid each site. Then ask:

- **Why should we avoid the sites we've talked about today, and sites like them?**
- **How can you make sure you avoid visiting Web sites like these?**
- **Is it tempting for you to visit any of the kinds of Web sites we've discussed? Why?**
- **If so, how can you resist the temptation?**
- **What does it mean to use the Internet wisely?**

Choose Your Closing

Option 1: Web Outreach

(For this activity you'll need markers, pencils, paper, and craft supplies.)

Say: **We've talked a lot about the negative things you can find on the Internet. But there are a lot of positive things you can find there too. What are some good things you can find on or do with the Internet?**

Allow kids to offer responses. Then say: **The Internet can be used to bring glory to God also. Let's design Web pages that would bring glory to Jesus.**

Have kids return to their groups of three. Give each group markers, pencils, paper, and craft supplies such as glitter and construction paper. Give groups about ten minutes to create models of Web pages that would bring glory to Jesus. Kids can put the home page on one sheet of paper and all the other pages on other sheets or just concentrate on the home page.

Have each group share and explain its Web site. Then ask:

- **What are some other ways to bring glory to God on the Internet?**
- **What will you do differently next time you go online?**
- **Do you have any other questions about how Christians should or should not use the Internet?**

Pray aloud for your students: **God, thank you for the tools we have such as computers and the Internet. There are so many dangers and so many opportunities online. We ask, God, that you would give us wisdom, that you would protect us, and that you would help us to glorify you when we go online. In Jesus' name, amen.**

Option 2: Repent and Be Saved

(Use this option if you have reason to believe that several of your students frequent inappropriate Web sites. You will need a Bible.)

Say: **We've seen that God wants us to keep our minds, our hearts, our eyes, our hands, and our entire lives pure and devoted to him. And we've seen some ways that the Internet can destroy that purity. So what do we do** now if we've already been dabbling with some of these inappropriate Web sites? **1 John 1:9 tells us.** Read this verse aloud.

Say: **God calls us to repentance and promises to forgive us when we come to him in true repentance. That means more than just telling God you're sorry for what you've done, but also committing to turn away from that action and not going back to it.**

One way to strengthen your commitment to stay away from these sites from now on is to confess to another person, such as a parent or another trusted adult. Then this person can help keep you accountable for not going back.

Ask your students to stand in a circle for prayer. Open the prayer yourself: **Dear Lord God, we come to you today in repentance for the inappropriate ways we have used the Internet. We want to be pure in all that we think, say, and do. Please forgive us. Listen to our silent prayers.** Give your students a few moments to pray silently. Then close the prayer: **Thank you, God, for your promise of forgiveness. Please help us to stay strong in our commitments to follow you. In Jesus' name, amen.**

Don't Go There!

www.totalcarnage!.com

This Web site features the latest shareware and freeware games of total carnage. Whether you're in the cockpit in T-970 or slugging through the swamp in Road Rage, you'll cause nothing but death and destruction. Log on at one of three levels of play: blood, guts, or total carnage.

www.win$money$.com

This Web site has it all. Play poker, blackjack, and online roulette. All you need is a credit card, and you can make lots of money. What are you waiting for? Come play now!

www.#hate#.com

If you're not one of us, you're one of them. We must be strong so *they* never hurt our way of life. Whatever we do, we must stop *them*.

www.*triple*X.com

This site has all the pictures of what you know you're not supposed to see.

www.+newagemovement+.com

This site helps you along your spiritual journey. Let go of the stale old Christian religion and embrace the light and freedom of the enlightened path.

www.^teentalk^.com

Get the latest gossip on all the stars. Who is being bad and what are they doing? We'll give you the latest photos they don't want you to see and the gossip they don't want you to hear. Find out what sensationally sinful thing they're doing now.

Goal:
To think about media choices.

Scripture Verses:
Romans 8:1-2, 6-9, 12-14;
Philippians 3:18-21;
1 Peter 5:8-11

Managing Media

Surf the Net. Listen to music. Watch television. Look at magazines. Play a video game. Preteens have almost unlimited media influences. And if parents or children *can* control the level of media influences at home, the minute a preteen steps into a friend's house, he or she is bombarded with an entirely different set of media possibilities.

Are your kids able to understand the media messages they see and hear? Are they able to grasp the importance of filtering messages that stand contrary to their Christian beliefs? Are they able to spot messages that can harm them? This lesson will help them do that, while creating a manifesto and a personal commitment time for students to promise to be careful about what they see and hear through the media.

Choose Your Opening

Option 1: Elite Marketing

(For this activity you will not need any supplies.)

Have kids get in groups of three.

Say: **I'd like for you to imagine that your group is an elite team of marketing executives based in New York City. Your team has been contracted to advertise a top-secret item to the public. I'd like you to think up an object to advertise.**

Give groups a few minutes to think up an object to market. When they're ready, say: **I'd like you to present your objects in an advertisement. Please create a fifteen-second sales pitch that you'll present to the company. There's one catch: You have to mime the presentation. Don't reveal what the object is that you're advertising; just give us the pitch, and we'll guess what you're trying to sell to us.**

When groups are ready, have each group come forward and present its marketing plan for the top-secret object. After each group presents its mime, ask students to guess what they think the group is selling. After a few students have guessed, ask the group to reveal what it's trying to sell. Repeat this process until each group has presented. Then say: **So much gets conveyed to us through the radio, television, and the Internet that we don't even realize it. If people tried to tell us stuff without using words or pictures, they wouldn't be very successful. Often the words that people use in the media, and the pictures they use to sell their stuff or send their message, can really hurt us. Let's talk about how we can make wise choices with the media that we encounter.**

Option 2: Wisdom Is...

(For this activity you'll need newsprint and markers.)

As students arrive, have them form groups of four. Give each group a sheet of newsprint and a marker.

Say: **Have you ever thought about wise people? There are a lot of them on the earth, and I'm sure there are some wise people in your life. I'd like you to make a list in your group of the wisest people you know.**

When groups have made their lists, say: **Now I'd like for you to think about what makes these people wise. What qualities do they have that make them wise? Write your ideas on the other side of your newsprint.**

As groups are writing their ideas, give each group another sheet of newsprint and several markers. When students are finished, say: **Now that you've made a list of the qualities of these wise people, I'd like for you to draw the wisest person in the world. Take all of the attributes that you just wrote down, and put them into one person. What might this person look like? As you draw this person, be sure to have an explanation of each characteristic you give him or her.**

When groups are finished, have each group come forward and share its wise-person drawing. As they share, be sure to ask students to give the reason for each characteristic that they drew. When all groups have presented, ask:

- **What makes someone wise?**
- **How can you tell that someone is wise?**
- **What kinds of decisions do wise people make?**
- **What choices might a wise person make about questionable media stuff such as movies or music?**

Say: **Today we're going to talk about how the media influence our lives. We're going to talk about how wise people handle the tough messages that some media influences send our way.**

The Bible Experience
· ·
Media Manifesto Part One

(For this activity you'll need copies of the "Media Messages Manifesto" handout on page 81, newsprint, tape, markers, paper, pencils, and Bibles.)

Have kids get into four equal-sized groups. Say: **Have you ever thought about the messages that the media send? How about the effect that the media and their messages have on your life? I'd like you to think about that for just a moment.**

Distribute paper and pencils, and have groups make a list of the messages that they feel the media send us. After a few minutes, have groups report their ideas. As they report, write their responses on a sheet of newsprint taped to the wall. Separate their ideas into the following two categories: "Positive Influences" and "Negative Influences."

When groups have finished, say: **All of these messages influence us in how we live and how we think.** Point to the negative influences. **These are really dangerous. Let's look at what the Bible says about these influences, and what we can do about them.**

Give each preteen a copy of the "Media Messages Manifesto" handout. Assign each group one of the passages from the handout to read. After groups have read the passages, have students write out what their passage means in the "What the Bible Says" column of their handouts. When they're finished, have students gather in the center of the classroom. Then say: **The Bible has a lot to say about how the media can influence us. I'd like for each group to read its passage aloud, then explain to us what it means. As groups share, please write down the responses in the appropriate box on your own handout.**

When groups have finished reading their passages and sharing their ideas, ask:

• **What does the Bible say we should do about messages that are harmful?**

• **Why does God want us not to allow those influences in our lives?**

• **What media influences can hurt us?**

• **How can these messages harm us?**

• **What do these messages hurt in us, our bodies or our minds?**

Say: **The Bible gives us a lot of really great direction about what to do with these messages. But how do we actually live that out? Let's work on that next.**

Reflection and Application
....
Media Manifesto Part Two

(For this activity you'll need Bibles, pencils, newsprint, a marker, and the copies of the "Media Messages Manifesto" handout.)

Say: **We've seen that the Bible has a lot to say about the choices we make. Let's look at how those ideas apply to our lives.**

Ask students to form four equal-sized groups with new students. Assign each group one of the passages from the handout. Explain to groups that you'd like for them to talk about how they can apply their passage to their lives, specifically in regards to the media. They should write their ideas in the "How I Can Apply It" section of their handouts. When they're finished, have students get together with another group and share their answers. Encourage students to write other groups' ideas in the appropriate places. When groups are finished, have them join with another group and trade responses. Repeat this until all the groups have met with each other. Then ask:

• **What are some things you learned from applying these passages to your life?**

• **Why is it important to live out what the Bible says about what we put in our brains?**

• **What are the effects of living out these ideas in our lives?**

• **What would our lives be like if we didn't filter out damaging media messages?**

Say: **I'd like for us to create a group commitment today. For the next few moments, think over the things you've read and heard.**

As students are thinking, hang a large sheet of newsprint on a wall of the classroom. Then say: **Now that you've thought, I'd like for us to create a group manifesto. This will be our group commitment about what we'll do when we hear wrong messages from any media.**

Lead kids in brainstorming their ideas by suggesting one to get them started:

"When I see something in a movie that doesn't glorify God, I'll turn off the movie, close my eyes, or walk away from what I'm seeing." Ask students to think up other ideas that relate specifically to particular media influences (music, the Internet, video games, magazines, and so on). When they're finished, read the manifesto aloud. Then say: **You've created something really great here. This is our group commitment to keep our minds and hearts pure.**

Invite students forward and ask them to sign the bottom of the manifesto. As they finish, encourage them to sit down.

Choose Your Closing

Option 1: My Media

(For this activity you'll need a Bible and modeling clay.)

Say: **You've seen that the Bible has a lot to say about the messages that we allow into our bodies, and you've helped create a cool commitment. But it's not that easy. Some of us really need help in giving up a particular influence in our lives.**

Ask students to find a place in the room where they can be alone. Give each student a piece of modeling clay. Ask students to form their clay into a shape that represents a commitment they would like to make after today's study. Students might say that they want to give up a particular media influence (students might form their clay into the shape of a television set), or that they'd like to be more careful about what they listen to on the radio (students might make an ear). When they're finished, have kids find a partner and explain their shapes.

When students are finished sharing, have them stand in a circle in the center of the meeting room. Ask volunteers to share their shapes with the entire class. Then say: **The Bible promises that if we give our sins to God, he will forgive us. He doesn't want to condemn us; he wants to free us!**

Read aloud Romans 8:1-2. Then ask students who wish to be free from their unhealthy media habits to drop their shapes on the floor in the middle of the circle. When students are finished, gather the shapes in your hands and begin kneading the clay together while explaining that God's forgiveness removes all our mistakes and cleans us. Close the meeting with a short prayer asking God to help your students resist media that aren't healthy.

Option 2: Media Filtering

(For this activity you'll need a Bible, newsprint, tape, and markers.)

Have kids find a place in the room where they can be alone. Then say: **You've discovered what the Bible says about these messages, and what we're supposed to do about them. I'd like for you to think about one area of media that you think might be damaging to your thinking.**

Write these words on a sheet of newsprint taped to the wall of the classroom: music, television, video games, Internet, magazines, movies. Explain to kids that you'd like for them to look over the list and think about these areas in their lives. Ask them to consider which area they feel is most dangerous for them. For example, students might realize that the music they listen to doesn't glorify God, or the video games they play have questionable content. After a few minutes, say: **I'd like for you to make a commitment today to be more careful about that problem area.**

Lay several markers on the floor underneath the newsprint. Ask students to come forward and make a mark next to the area where they'd like to be more careful. When students are finished, say: **Today you've not only drafted a group manifesto committing to what media messages you will allow in your life, but you've also committed to be extra careful with certain areas that are weak points for you. That's great!**

Read Romans 8:1-2 aloud. Then say: **God promises that when we lay something at his feet, he doesn't condemn us. He forgives us, and he frees us.**

Have students pray silently for strength to be careful about the media choices they make. Close the meeting with a short prayer asking God to help your students keep their commitments.

Media Messages Manifesto

What the Bible Says:　　　　　How I Can Apply It:

Romans 8:6-9

....　　　..

Romans 8:12-14

....　　　..

Philippians 3:18-21

....　　　..

1 Peter 5:8-11

....　　　..

God's Green Earth

Your preteen kids are at an age when it's relatively easy to get them fired up about issues and causes. Use today's lesson to get them on fire for the cause of caring for God's creation. Be honest about the facts, but be careful not to frighten or overwhelm your students with the problems in the environment. Be sure to help your kids brainstorm plenty of realistic options that they can pursue to make a real difference. If they think the problem is too big for them to change, they will be less likely to even try to be part of a solution.

Choose Your Opening

Option 1: All God's Creatures

(For this activity you will need copies of the "God's Amazing Creatures" handout on page 85 and pencils.)

Say: **Welcome, class! Today we're going to have a true-or-false quiz.**

Wait until the groans subside, then say: **But this will be a really off-the-wall, different kind of a test, and I think you'll find it a lot of fun. And, if you'd like, you may work with another person or in small groups.**

Pass out pencils and the copies of the quiz, and give kids a few minutes to go over the questions. Then go through the questions with the whole group, reading a question aloud and asking kids to call out their answers. You might also ask them to explain why they think the statement is true or false. Here's the answer key: All of the statements are true! (#9—The tree climbers are the big robber crab and the mudskipper fish.)

Say: **Today we're going to learn even more about God's amazing creation and what we can do to take better care of it.**

Option 2: Let's Make an Earth!

(You will need a copy of the "Let's Make an Earth!" handout on page 86 for each of the participants.)

Ask for volunteers for a skit, and distribute copies of the handout to each of your participants. Explain to them that stage directions are given in parentheses. Have your students read and act out the skit. When they're finished, give everyone a huge round of applause.

Say: **Today we're going to take at look at how people have done so far in caring for God's creation, and we'll explore some ways that we can improve our record.**

The Creator

(For this activity you will need Bibles.)

Ask for volunteers to read these verses aloud: Genesis 1:11-12, 20-21; 2:8-9.

Say: **God planted a garden, and created all living things.**

Ask:

• **Why do you think God did this?**

Have a volunteer read Genesis 1:26-29 aloud. Ask:

• **Have you ever created anything that you were really proud of?**

Say: **It's fun to be able to tell about these things.**

Give kids plenty of time to share. Then ask:

• **What's your most creative time: morning, afternoon, or night?**

• **What do you think God's most creative time is?**

• **Do you think God is proud of the things he created?**

• **Did you ever have someone damage or ruin something you created? How did that make you feel?**

• **God told Adam to take care of his creation—the environment. How do you think God feels about the way we're doing that job?**

Ask a volunteer to read aloud Genesis 2:19-20a. Ask:

• **How do you choose names for your pets?**

• **What do you think it would have been like to be Adam and to choose names for all the birds and animals?**

• **How long do you think it would take you to name all the birds and animals in our world?**

• **How do you feel about people you know, and how is that different from how you feel about total strangers?**

• **If people knew the names of every kind of bird and animal, how do you think it would affect the way we treat them?**

Reflection and Application

God Is Sad

(For this activity you will need pencils, paper, white board, and a marker.)

Have kids get into groups of three or four and discuss things we're doing to our environment that might make God sad. On paper, have them list at least three of these things. After sufficient time, have groups share their lists.

Write students' ideas on a white board as they share. If any group repeats an idea that another group has already shared, keep track of the number of times each idea is mentioned.

Say: **This list can look pretty overwhelming. What can we do to help? Let's find out how we can make a difference.**

Facts

Even though we've been working at cleaning up our environment for the past thirty years, pollutants are still causing problems in our environment. Here are some facts you can use to help kids understand:

• Global warming, acid rain, reduction of the ozone layer, and overpopulation are all threats to the food supply and to good health.

• Auto emissions legislation has provided some relief, but the fact is that there is a constantly growing number of automobiles in the world today. Plus, Third World countries have developed added industry, which enhances the problem.

• Our forests are shrinking, soils are being eroded away, and there is more desert every year.

• Acid rain is caused by sulfur dioxide and nitrogen oxides in the upper atmosphere, which are converted to two acids: sulfuric and nitric. These then can be carried by air currents for hundreds of miles and have a devastating impact on crops and water supplies.

• Global warming is a threat that can be diminished through reduction of the use of fossil fuels.

Option 1: Every Little Bit Helps

(For this activity you will need a white board and a marker.)

Refer to the suggestions that your small groups shared in the Reflection and Application activity. Share with them that it's good to be aware of these things, but it's even better to do something about these problems.

Have kids brainstorm ways that they could help. Kids might choose to do projects on pollution and the environment for school. Or they could simply get their own families to start recycling. Other practical ideas include turning off lights and appliances when they're not in use; and carpooling or even walking, bicycling, or taking a bus when possible. Write kids' ideas on the white board as they brainstorm.

Ask your kids to make a commitment to do one thing to help fulfill God's desire for us to care for his planet Earth. This can be done by a simple show of hands for the ideas kids are willing to try.

Close class in prayer, thanking God for the beautiful creation we see all around us. Ask him to help your students to better care for his world.

Option 2: Letter Writing

(For this activity you will need paper, pencils, and envelopes. You should also be prepared with mailing information for your newspaper, local politicians, and local corporations.)

Distribute paper and pencils. Explain to kids that one way they can get involved in helping the environment is by writing a letter to the editor of your newspaper. Many people read these letters, so it is a good way to educate the public and stir them to action. Another way to help is to write letters to large companies that do not follow good environmental policies, or to government officials, making them aware of environmental problems and your students' concerns. Come prepared with the names and addresses of your local senator and members of congress, plus your newspaper's editorial information and a telephone book for other addresses.

Help your kids get started by offering them some pointers. They should first decide on the issue they want to write about. Next they should decide who to write their letter to. Encourage students to clearly state in their letters what the problem is and what causes that problem. They should also include the results of this environmental problem. Finally, kids should offer some suggestions for change, what people can do to fix this problem. When kids are finished, collect their letters and promise to mail them this week. Then do it!

Share with kids that it is also important to pray for our legislators, other government officials, and business owners. Ask kids if they think God would want us to pray about the issues we've been discussing today. Close in prayer for these people to become more aware of the need to care for God's green earth. Thank God for his beautiful creation, and ask that your students will also become better caretakers of the earth.

God's Amazing Creatures

1. A tree frog has feet like suction cups and can walk upside down on a ceiling.

2. In addition to the brown earthworms, there are worms that look like feather dusters, shoelaces, knots, tangled red ribbons, and even worms that are flat and tumble like leaves.

3. These are all animal names: aye-aye, bongo, bush baby, puku, numbat, sassaby, shou, po-toroo, wallaroo, wapiti, wallaby, softly-softly, and squeaker.

4. There is a monkey called a monkey-monkey monkey.

5. And there is a fish called a Hippoglossus hippoglossus, and other fish called scat, scup, snook, silver dollar, snaggle tooth, lookdown, puffer, and grunt.

6. There is a fish you can play ball with. It's a puffer fish and can puff itself into a ball.

7. Cormorants are birds that swim under water.

8. Umas are lizards that swim in sand.

9. There is a fish and there is a crab that can both climb trees.

10. Sometimes tiny specks of dust are actually animals.

11. The feathers on a duck are waterproof.

12. Water skaters are bugs that skate on top of the water.

13. Salmon live in salt water for their whole lives—except that they are born in fresh water, and they die in fresh water.

14. A rhinoceros can have its own security system. It's a tick-bird, which sits on the back of the rhinoceros. When danger is near, the bird warns the rhinoceros by flapping its wings and making loud noises.

15. An earthworm moves through the ground by digging tunnels. To get rid of the dirt it digs, it just eats it.

(Information taken from *Childcraft: The How and Why Library.* © 1965 Field Enterprises Educational Corporation.)

Let's Make an Earth!

Characters: Narrator, God, Man, trees, bushes, puppy dog, ostrich, fish
(Note: Instructions are in parentheses.)

Narrator: In the beginning, God created the heavens and the earth.

God: I'm gonna make land. LAND! Hmm. That's GOOD.

Narrator: Then he created all the plants and trees.

God: OK. Now some PLANTS. *(Bush walks in on knees—holds arms up like branches.)* Not bad. OK. Trees. *(Trees are taller and hold arms up high.)* More bushes. *(More bushes enter.)* They look a little empty. I know! Fruit! That's GOOD.

Narrator: But the fruit was going to waste. So God made birds.

God: Hmm. All that fruit's falling on the ground. Need something to eat it up. BIRDS! *(Ostrich enters.)*

Narrator: Then he made animals.

God: ANIMALS! *(Puppy dog enters, barking.)*

Narrator: And fish.

God: FISH! *(Fish comes in, but everybody knows fish don't make any sounds. OK, maybe a blub-blub.)*

Narrator: And he said it was GOOD.

God: That's GOOD.

Narrator: But God wanted someone more like him.

God: OK. I'm getting all the lines. That is, if you just ignore the Narrator—which is a good idea, actually. I need someone else in the skit.

Narrator: So he decided to make Man.

God: I know! I'll make someone like me. MAN! *(Man enters and lies down on the floor.)* Whew! That's VERY GOOD!

Man: *(Lying on the floor. Gets up like he's just waking up.)* Hmm. Good morning, God. *(Stands up, looks around.)* Wow! Look at all these plants and animals and birds and fish and stuff. Wow! *(Plants and trees shake. Critters run around making their noises.)*

God: Yeah. Cool, huh?

Man: What do you call them, God?

God: Call them? I don't call them. They just come.

Man: No. I meant to say, what are their names?

God: Hey, I spent all week creating them. When did I have time to name them?

Man: Well, they need names.

Narrator: Now, God had done all the creating, so he figured it was Man's turn to do something. So he decided to let Man come up with all the names.

God: OK, then YOU name them!

Man: I can do that. *(Points at each one.)* German shepherd, trout, ostrich…

God: *(Interrupts)* But after you've named them, you need to take care of them.

Man: Of course I'll do that.

God: But I mean REALLY take care of them. *(Critters and plants kind of snuggle up to God.)*

Man: I SAID I can do that.

God: That means you have to take care of their food supply and their environment too—the air and the water.

Man: I can do that, too. I'll take care of them all. *(Critters smile, plants bounce and act happy.)*

Narrator: Now, back then, it was pretty easy to take care of the environment, cause there weren't many people, and there were no cars, or toxic waste, or things like that.

God: That means you need to be really careful about things like factories and cars and trucks, and chemicals.

Man: Well, I guess I can do that, too.

God: What if that means that you can't have computers or toys, or your fruit has spots on it?

Man: Hey, God, let's not push this thing too far.

Hope for the Hopeless

Preteen kids are generally pretty self-absorbed. They think about themselves, their friends, and their families, but don't generally think much beyond their immediate contacts. In this lesson you will help your students think about people in the rest of the world who do not have all the "stuff" and all the privileges that your students enjoy. Just awakening an awareness in your kids that there are hurting people in the world is a tremendous first step. In this lesson you will also help your kids take their concerns a step further and get involved in helping other people.

Choose Your Opening

Option 1: What Would I Miss?

(For this activity you will need a white board, marker, paper, and pencils.)

In this activity you'll try to help kids get in touch with what it means to live without hope. Begin by passing out paper and pencils. Write these words on a white board or other place where kids can see them: poverty, homelessness, war, famine, earthquake, hurricane, flood.

Say: **Today we're going to begin by thinking about the things that we have. Think about the things in your home and your school that are important to you, and those that make your life more comfortable. They can be possessions, people, animals, furniture, or even things like heat and lights and running water.**

Give kids three to five minutes to make their lists. Then say: **Now I want you to choose one of the words from the list I've written on the board. Write the word that you've chosen on the top of your paper. Look at the list you just wrote, and cross out the things that you could lose if this happened to you. For example, if you were poor, would you have all the things on your list? Which ones might you not have? If there were a hurricane or flood in our town, what might you lose, or what might be hurt or damaged? Those are the things you should cross off your list.**

Give kids a few minutes, then say: **Next to the things still on your list, write down how they might be changed if the word you chose happened to you. For example, pets or people might be lost, your house might be without power or water, your room might be gone.**

After a few minutes, say: **We started with so many things on our lists, but because of one little word, most of us are left with almost nothing on our lists, except maybe some things that have been ruined or damaged. We are used to living with everything that was on our original lists, but believe it or not, most people in the world live with something more like what's on your**

final list. Have students hold on to their lists for future use later in this lesson.

Option 2: Who's Hurting?

(For this activity you will need scissors, highlighters, newspapers, a white board, marker, and a plastic trash bag.)

Pass out scissors, highlighters, and news sections from a large daily newspaper. Write these words on the white board or someplace else where everyone can see: poverty, homelessness, war, famine, earthquake, hurricane, flood.

Say: **Sometimes it's easy to just accept the world around us as we see it. In fact, that's pretty normal. But today I want us to see if we can look at the world around us as Jesus sees it. Let's start by looking for these words in the newspaper. When you find one, highlight it and cut out the article. Get in a group of three or four, and let's see which group can come up with the most articles, and which group can come up with the most highlighted key words.**

Give groups about five minutes to search their newspapers, then pass around a large plastic trash bag for all the sections of newspaper they did not use. Have students keep the articles they did use for future use later in this lesson. Have a show of hands to determine which group had the most articles and which found the most key words. Give each group a minute to share what they found.

Say: **These tragedies are things that we probably don't think about very often, but many people in the world have no choice but to think about them because of the way these tragedies have affected their lives.**

The Bible Experience

The Good Samaritan

(For this activity you will need Bibles.)

This activity helps kids get in touch with the human drama in the story Jesus told about the good Samaritan. You will read the story from Luke 10:25-37, and have kids act out the parts. They can do this in pantomime, or if you have some actors and actresses in the group, let them actually repeat the lines that you're reading and/or make appropriate sounds. Appropriate noises might include expressions of the victim's pain, the robbers' beating, the dismay of the priest and the Levite, and the concern of the Samaritan.

Say: **I'm going to read a Bible story, and I need some help in acting it out.** Recruit and assign the parts you need: Jesus, Law Expert, Victim, Robbers, Priest, Levite, Samaritan, Innkeeper. **As I read about your character, please come up to the front and do whatever is being described in the Scripture I'm reading. For example, we'll start with Jesus and the law expert, and they'll stand here at the front. Each time I read something that their character said, they will repeat it. Each of you will do the same with your characters. I'll pause and give you time to do that. If you don't have lines, you may make appropriate sounds and actions. For example, the victim might groan, and the robbers might say things such as, "Give me your money!"** Give instructions where kids

Leader Tip

For a few nights prior to teaching this lesson, keep a blank videotape in your VCR and try to record parts of some news stories about the key words: poverty, homelessness, war, famine, earthquake, hurricane, flood. Use these as a visual tool to help kids focus in on the pain that these things cause to people.

are to stand and when they are to enter.

Say: **When I've finished with your part, you may stand over at the side until the Scripture is completed.** Read the Scripture, pausing to give plenty of time for kids to act out their parts. If you have kids who are not in the drama, have them follow along in their Bibles. Or add parts such as additional robbers, workers at the inn (who can gawk and stare and make comments), a crowd around the lawyer, a priest's assistant, and so on.

When you've finished, give everybody a big round of applause, and let them go back to their seats. Say: **Now, let's turn in our Bibles to the story I've just read from Luke 10:25-37.** Wait a moment until everybody has the passage. **Let's take a look at the priest and the Levite in verses 31 and 32.**

Read those two verses again. Ask:

• **Why do you think the priest and Levite acted the way they did?**

Say: **Let's look at verses 33 through 35.**

Have a volunteer read these verses aloud. Ask:

• **What did the Samaritan do?**

Say: **Jews and Samaritans hated each other, just as some races still hate each other today.**

Ask:

• **Why do you suppose Jesus used a hated Samaritan in this story to be the one to care for the victim?**

• **How did the Samaritan pay for the victim's needs? The answer is in verse 35.**

• **Wasn't that a bit much? Why do you think the man didn't simply call the police or just take the man to the hospital? Why did he actually pay the guy's bill?**

Have a volunteer read verse 36 aloud. Then repeat the question Jesus asked:

• **Which of these three do you think was a neighbor to the man who fell into the hands of robbers?**

• **What did Jesus tell the man to do at the end of verse 37?**

• **How can we do what Jesus said to the man: "Go and do likewise"?**

• **If there were a famine or a hurricane or a flood in our town, what might you be able to do to be a good neighbor to others?**

Say: **Let's go back to verse 29.** Ask for a volunteer to read that verse aloud. Jesus told the story of the good Samaritan as an answer to the young law expert's question: **"And who is my neighbor?"**

Reflection and Application

Who's My Neighbor?

(For this activity you will need props for food, a drinking glass, clothing or a blanket, and books. Or you may simply have students pantomime the props. You will also need copies of the "Sheep and Goats Skit" handout on page 92.)

Say: **We're going to read another story from the Bible, one that gives us lots of ideas about how we can be good neighbors. It's found in Matthew 25:31-46. Once again, I'll need some help.**

Leader Tip

There are several dynamics in this story, many of which still apply today. The victim was almost certainly a Jew. The Samaritans were considered second-class citizens and were hated by the Jews. The priest and the Levite may have feared a plot, been afraid the robbers would come after them if they hung around, or had concerns about touching someone injured or dead who would make them "unclean."

The lawyer was an expert in the Law of Moses, and most likely not sincere in his question. The question was meant to trick Jesus, and Jesus knew all of this as he responded.

A few facts about homelessness in the United States might be helpful to have at your fingertips.

• Some homeless people are employed full-time or part-time, but can't afford housing.

• Homeless people include children, disabled vets, the elderly, and AIDS victims.

• Many homeless children are both homeless and without parents.

• By 1993, there were more than three million people who were homeless at least one night per year.

• Illegal immigrants are often living on our streets without homes.

• Many homeless people have completed high school. Some of them even went to college.

(Information taken from *54 Ways You Can Help the Homeless*, by Rabbi Charles A. Kroloff. © 1993 Hugh Lauter Levin Associates, Inc. and Behrman House, Inc.)

Recruit one or more students for each of the following parts: righteous (sheep), unrighteous (goats), hungry people, thirsty people, naked people, strangers, sick people, prisoners. For large groups, you can also add the devil and his angels. With smaller groups, just let the story refer to them, and have students double up on roles. You should be the Reader. Read aloud Matthew 25:31-34 to introduce the skit.

Following the skit, ask kids to share what they think they should and could do to help people who need hope. Ask:

• **Thinking about the story of the good Samaritan, how would you answer the question: Who's my neighbor?**

• **Who are "the least of these brothers" of Jesus?**

• **If there were a famine or a hurricane or a flood in Ecuador or Egypt or France, how could you be a good neighbor?**

• **What about homeless or poor people right here in our own country? How could you be a good neighbor to them?**

Help your students brainstorm ways that they can be helpful to their neighbors who are in need. Think about the homeless, sick people, poor people, people who have survived natural disasters or been victims of crime, and so on.

Choose Your Closing

Option 1: What Do People Need?

(Use this option if you used Choose Your Opening Option 1. You will need the lists students made in the opening activity, pencils, a white board, and a marker.)

Say: **Look back over the lists you made at the beginning of class.**
Ask:

• **What things on those lists do you think people might need if their town had experienced a hurricane or tornado or flood?**

• **What about people in a country that has been devastated by famine? What things on your lists would they be missing?**

• **What about homeless people right here in our country or city—what things on your list might they be living without?**

Say: **In small groups of three or four, brainstorm what you might be able to do to "be a good neighbor." Make a list on the back of your paper.**

After a few minutes of brainstorming, have groups share their ideas with the class. Write their ideas on a white board. Ideas might include volunteering at a soup kitchen or homeless shelter; giving away some of their clothes, toys, or food; giving money to organizations that help people in need; visiting people in hospitals or nursing homes; or volunteering with their families for organizations such as Habitat for Humanity or the American Red Cross.

Encourage your students to consider following up on one or more of the ideas mentioned. Close class in prayer, thanking God for the many blessings he has given us, and asking him to use your students to bring help and comfort to hurting people.

Option 2: Hope for the Hopeless

(Use this option if you used Choose Your Opening Option 2. You will need the newspaper articles from the opening option, a white board, and a marker.)

Say: **Take a look at the articles you cut out of the newspaper.** Give kids a moment to get them back out and look at them. Give them an opportunity to restate what their articles were about. Focusing on one article at a time, ask:

* **What would it mean to be a good neighbor to these people?**
* **What would these people need?**

After everyone has had a chance to go over his or her articles, say: **Jesus said we should go and do as the good Samaritan did.**

Ask:

* **What could you do to make a difference in these people's lives and be a good neighbor to them?**

As kids give answers, write them on a white board. Ideas might include volunteering at a soup kitchen or homeless shelter; giving away some of their clothes, toys, or food; giving money to organizations that help people in need; visiting people in hospitals or nursing homes; or volunteering with their families for organizations such as Habitat for Humanity or the American Red Cross.

Encourage your students to consider following up on one or more of the ideas mentioned. Close class in prayer, thanking God for the many blessings he has given us, and asking him to use your students to bring help and comfort to hurting people.

Sheep and Goats Skit
(Matthew 25:31-46)

Reader: "For I was hungry *(the hungry people beg)*

Reader: and you gave me something to eat *(the sheep give them food)*,

Reader: I was thirsty *(the thirsty people look thirsty)*

Reader: and you gave me something to drink *(the sheep give them some water)*,

Reader: I was a stranger *(the strangers act strange)*

Reader: and you invited me in *(the sheep open the door)*,

Reader: I needed clothes *(the naked people try to cover themselves)*

Reader: and you clothed me *(the sheep give them clothes)*,

Reader: I was sick and you looked after me *(the sheep care for the sick people)*,

Reader: I was in prison and you came to visit me. *(The sheep read books to the prisoners.)*

Reader: Then the righteous will answer him, "Lord, when did we see you hungry and feed you, or thirsty and give you something to drink? When did we see you a stranger and invite you in, or needing clothes and clothe you? When did we see you sick or in prison and go to visit you?" *(The sheep hold their hands up and look inquisitive.)*

Reader: The King will reply, "I tell you the truth, whatever you did for one of the least of these brothers of mine, you did for me."

Reader: Then he will say to those on his left, "Depart from me, you who are cursed, into the eternal fire prepared for the devil and his angels. *(If you have these characters, they can stand to the side and beckon people to a pretend fire.)*

Reader: For I was hungry and you gave me nothing to eat *(the goats eat the food and let the hungry starve)*,

Reader: I was thirsty and you gave me nothing to drink *(goats hog all the water)*,

Reader: I was a stranger and you did not invite me in *(goats slam the door in the faces of the strangers)*,

Reader: I needed clothes and you did not clothe me *(goats keep all the clothes)*,

Reader: I was sick and in prison and you did not look after me." *(Goats play games and ignore the sick and imprisoned.)*

Reader: They also will answer, "Lord, when did we see you hungry or thirsty or a stranger or needing clothes or sick or in prison, and did not help you?" *(Goats hold hands up and look inquisitive.)*

Reader: He will reply, "I tell you the truth, whatever you did not do for one of the least of these, you did not do for me."

Reader: Then they will go away to eternal punishment, but the righteous to eternal life. *(Goats go over to the devil and his angels and act like they're suffering. Sheep go to eternal life.)*

Section 5:
• • • • • • • • • •
Committed to Christ

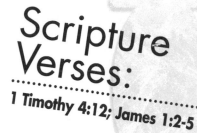

Standing Up in School

Preteen kids are very conscious of their friends' opinions. They want to be liked, and greatly fear rejection. That makes it difficult for them to stand up for beliefs that are not popular. They need help in seeing that they can have an impact on their friends for God. God will help them and give them the courage they need to stand up for what is right.

Choose Your Opening

Option 1: A Tough Decision

(For this activity you'll need pencils and note cards.)

After kids have arrived, give each one a note card and a pencil. Then read them the following scenario:

You are the captain on a starship. You've just encountered the enemy and escaped, but barely. Two crew members were taken by the enemy. Your ship is severely damaged, but you feel you can outrun your enemies if you leave immediately. Several crew members have advised you to run while you can, but you can't help but think of what's happening to your lost crew members. You'd like to go back and rescue them. Thinking for only a few seconds, you make your decision. You say...

Tell kids to write their responses on their note cards. When they're finished, have them read what they wrote. Ask:

• **How is this like standing up for what you know is right at school?**

• **What kinds of things make it tough to stand up as a Christian at school?**

Say: **Sometimes it's tough to stand up and do what's right. Today we're going to be looking at how we can do that in our lives at school.**

Option 2: Blow the Man Down

(For this activity you'll need toothpicks and modeling clay.)

Have kids form groups of three or four. Give each group a small piece of modeling clay and about six or eight toothpicks. Say: **Using only these supplies, make a character that stands at least six inches tall, and make sure it can stand up on its own.**

Give kids a few minutes to create their characters, then say: **Now we're going to see how well these characters can stand up to some pressure. Without touching anyone else's character in any way, go around to other groups' characters and see if you can blow them over.**

Allow groups to go around and see if they can blow over other groups' characters. Congratulate those whose characters remain standing. Ask:

- **How did you feel when your character remained standing or fell?**
- **How is this like when you try to stand up as a Christian at school?**

Then say: **I didn't tell you when you made your characters that they were going to have to stand up to someone blowing on them, so some of you weren't prepared for them to face that pressure. Today, we're going to talk about being prepared to stand up against pressure when it's hard to do what's right.**

The Bible Experience

Being an Example

(For this activity you'll need a Bible, paper, and pencils.)

Ask:

- **In what ways do people look down on you?**
- **How does that make you feel?**
- **What can you do to keep people from looking down on you?**

Say: **The Bible lets us know one way you can keep others from looking down on you even though you're young. Let's read 1 Timothy 4:12.**

Read the verse aloud, and then form five groups. A group can be as small as one person. Say: **Pretend your groups are research teams. This verse says you can avoid being looked down on by being an example. I'm going to assign each group one area in which this verse tells us to be an example. Your team's assignment is to come up with ways you can be an example in that area.**

Assign each research team one of the following areas: in speech, in life, in love, in faith, and in purity. Give students pencils and paper, and have each group write down at least five ways a preteen can be an example to others in the area they've been assigned. Allow about five minutes, and then have groups report what they've written. Then ask:

- **How is being this kind of an example like the "standing up" we talked about in our opening activity?**
- **What effect might being this kind of an example have on other kids at school?**
- **How easy is it to do these things?**
- **What can help us stand up when it's not easy?**

Say: **God doesn't just tell us that we should be examples, but he also helps us do that.**

Read aloud James 1:2-5. Ask:

- **What does this verse say about the help we can have when we want to stand up in tough times?**
- **How do we get that help?**
- **What does wisdom have to do with it?**

Say: **When it's tough to be an example at school, we can be sure we'll have God's help if we ask for it. And God is wanting and waiting for us to ask, because he wants us to succeed at standing up as Christians at school.**

Standing in Tough Situations

(For this activity you'll need newsprint and markers.)

Give each group a sheet of newsprint and a marker. Say: **As a team, brainstorm two situations in which it would be tough for you to stand up and be a good example at school. Briefly describe each situation on your newsprint. If you prefer, you may draw the situations. Be ready to explain them to the class.**

After a few minutes for thinking and writing or drawing, have teams report on their situations. If you're short on time, just have each team report on what they think is the tougher of their two situations. After each situation is presented, ask your class members to suggest ways to make it easier to stand up and be a good example in that situation.

After all have shared and suggestions have been made, say: **No matter how tough the situation, you can be a good example. And God will be there to help you.**

Choose Your Closing

Option 1: Getting God's Help

(For this activity you will not need any supplies.)

Have kids form pairs. Say: **One way we can be prepared to stand up when things get tough is to ask God right now to be with us. In your pairs, pray for each other. Ask God to help your partner when things get tough to be the example God wants him or her to be. Consider committing to praying for each other throughout this week and checking in with each other to see how it's going.**

Allow a few minutes for kids to pray, and then close this session with your own prayer, asking God to give kids the wisdom and courage they need to stand up as Christians at school.

Option 2: Ways to Stand

(For this activity you will need the lists of ways to be examples that students made during the "Bible Experience" activity.)

Have kids look back at the findings of their original research groups. Have each group read again what it means to be an example "in speech, in life, in love, in faith, and in purity."

Have kids reflect silently on the following questions:

• **How are you doing in each of these areas?**

• **What areas do you really need to work on?**

Say: **God will help you improve in these areas if you ask for his help. Choose at least one of these areas in which you really want God to help you be a better example. Commit to seeking his help and trying to do better this week.**

Close your session with prayer, asking God to help your kids lean on his help when they need to stand up for him in tough situations.

A Praying Person

Preteen kids are at a point in life when they're beginning to develop what may be lifelong patterns. As difficult as it sometimes is to maintain, personal devotional time with God is critical to a growing relationship with him. Use this session to help kids see the benefit of getting started with that devotional time now, so that it will be a habit they are glad to maintain in the difficult years that are still to come.

Choose Your Opening

Option 1: Best Friends

(For this activity you will not need any supplies.)

Say: **In a minute I'm going to ask you a couple of questions. I want you to think of answers to them, but don't tell anyone. Keep the answers in your mind. Here are the questions.**

Ask:

• **Of all your friends, who do you like best?**

• **Of all your friends, who do you spend the most time with?**

Allow kids to think for a minute, then say: **If the answer to both of those questions was the same person, raise your hand.**

After looking around at all the hands, say: **I've got one more question for you.**

Ask:

• **If you could spend even more time with that person, would you want to do it?**

After getting kids' answers, say: **God wants us to be in a close relationship with him. We've seen that we enjoy spending time with people we like. But as Christians, we often don't spend a lot of time building our relationships with God, even though we say we love him. Today we're going to be looking at what it takes to keep that relationship with God growing.**

Option 2: Prayer Creations

(For this activity you'll need paper, markers, and art supplies.)

Give preteens paper, markers, and any other available art supplies. Say: **Today we're going to be talking about prayer. To get us started thinking about prayer, I'd like for you to draw or create something that shows what prayer means to you.**

Let kids use any of the art supplies they want to make their creations. Allow several minutes for them to work, then have each individual show and explain what he or she has created. Say: **We all have different ideas and feelings about prayer. Today we're going to look specifically at how we can make prayer a more consistent part of our lives.**

The Bible Experience
Pray Continually

(For this activity you'll need paper, pencils, Bibles, newsprint, and markers.)

Have preteens form pairs. Then have partners go to opposite ends of the room. Have all of your students close their eyes and mingle with the others at their end of the room. Say: **When I say "go," I want you to start walking toward the other end of the room with your eyes closed. Your goal is to find your partner. You may call out your partner's name once every five seconds. You must keep your eyes closed the whole time.**

Say "go," and let kids find their partners. Make sure they're pausing for at least five seconds between calling out their partners' names.

After kids have found their partners, have each student choose a new partner. Separate them to opposite ends of the room again. Have them close their eyes and mingle again. Then say: **When I say "go," head for the other end of the room to find your partner—only this time you can call out your partner's name as often as you want.**

Say "go," and let kids find their partners. Then gather students together and discuss the following questions. Ask:

• **How were the two times we did this activity different?**

• **Why was it easier the second time?**

Have kids turn in their Bibles and read 1 Thessalonians 5:17. Ask:

• **How is praying continually similar to what we did in the second part of the activity we just did?**

• **Which part of the activity is like the way many Christians pray?**

• **Why do we pray?**

Form groups of three or four and have students read together Philippians 4:6-7. Give groups paper and pencils, and have them write down all the benefits of prayer they see in those verses of Scripture. Allow about three minutes for groups to discuss the passage, then have them report what they discovered. List their responses on a sheet of newsprint. Then ask:

• **What difference can prayer make in our lives?**

• **What difference can prayer make in our relationships with God?**

Say: **Praying not only helps us receive the things we need, but it also helps us have peace in our lives as we develop a closer relationship with God. Prayer is one way we can let go of all our worries and give them up to God, leaving only God's peace to guard our hearts and minds. Prayer is also a great way to say thanks to God for all that he has given us and done for us.**

Leader Tip

Be sure to clear all chairs, desks, and other potential hazards out of students' way before you attempt this activity. Monitor students closely to be sure that nobody gets hurt.

When to Pray

(For this activity you will need Bibles.)

In their groups, have preteens read Mark 1:35. Then have them discuss with their partners the following questions. Ask:

- **Why did Jesus need to pray?**
- **Why do you think Jesus went out early in the morning to pray?**
- **What ideas might this verse give us about how we should pattern our personal times of prayer?**

Have groups report on their discussions. Then say: **Jesus went out early in the morning to be alone to pray. If even Jesus, who was God himself, needed that time to be alone with the Father, how much more do we need times of prayer like that! God wants each of us to build our relationship with him by spending time with him in prayer. For many people, early morning is a good time to do that. Others spend time in prayer at bedtime. Those times are good, and we need those times alone, but as we studied earlier, the Bible also says we're to pray continually.**

Ask:

- **How can we do that?**

Allow several kids to volunteer answers, and then say: **We can pray continually by always having our relationship with God in the front of our minds. When our minds are not occupied with things we need to consciously think about or do, we can be thinking about what God might want us to do, and about what God has done for us. In that way we can be connecting with him in our thoughts much of the time. And that's what God would like for us to do. He'd like for us to be so in love with him that we think about him all the time.**

Choose Your Closing

Option 1: Prayer Circle

(For this activity you will not need any supplies.)

Gather your group in a big circle. Say: **We've been talking a lot about prayer today. Now we're going to spend some time praying. We're going to pray together, allowing anyone here in the circle to pray aloud for anything you want to. You might want to thank God for something he's done for you, or ask God to help you in some area of prayer we've talked about. Or you might want to ask God to help with a special need in your life or in some situation you know about. Feel free to pray about anything you want—just be sure your prayer won't be embarrassing to someone here. Everyone should also be praying silently even when no one is praying aloud.**

Have students close their eyes and pray. Don't give up too quickly on having kids pray aloud. Remain silent for at least three minutes even if no one prays aloud. Then close your prayer time and the session with your own prayer.

Option 2: Prayer Partners

(For this activity you will not need any supplies.)

Have kids form pairs. Say: **The person you're paired with is going to be your prayer partner for the next week. I'd like for you to pray for each other every day this week, and to contact each other either by phone, e-mail, or in person sometime this week to ask how your prayer lives are going. Be encouraging to each other, and maybe even try to get together to pray sometime during the week. Right now, share with your partner things you'd appreciate prayer for. I'll give you two minutes to share prayer needs with each other, and then I'm going to ask you to pray together.**

Give kids two minutes for sharing, and then tell them it's time to pray. When it appears that most pairs are finishing praying, pray aloud a closing prayer to wrap up your session.

Servant Serving

Preteen kids struggle with seeing other kids their age as "better" than they are—kids who can play a sport better, kids who are more attractive, kids who are smarter, kids who are more popular. The result is that many preteen kids don't think they have much to offer. However, the Bible points out that God values and gives gifts to each of us. Just because someone is not an athlete, a brain, or a fashion model doesn't mean that person doesn't have God-given gifts to serve him. Help your kids understand that serving God is something that each of us can do, and that God has given each of us special abilities for doing just that.

Choose Your Opening

Option 1: Giving Gifts

(For this activity you will need note cards and pencils.)

Have students form pairs. Say: **For the next minute, the partner in your pair who is closer to me will tell the other partner about what he or she likes to do and would like to do for a living as an adult. Go.**

After one minute, have partners switch roles. After another minute, distribute note cards and pencils. Say: **Now I want you to think about what special ability would help your partner accomplish what he or she wants to do as an adult. Write on your note card, "If I could, I would give you the gift of..." and then finish your sentence. For example, if your partner wanted to be an artist, you might write, "If I could, I would give you the gift of creative artistic ability."**

When kids have written their cards, have them give them to their partners. Then say: **Unfortunately, we can't really give such gifts to each other. But God can! In this lesson we're going to look at the gifts God gives us and how we can use them to serve him.**

Option 2: Putting Gifts to Use

(For this activity you will need to prepare "gifts" for your students before class. Write the gifts mentioned in Romans 12:6-8 on separate slips of paper. Make as many copies as you need so that every preteen will get one slip. Wrap the slips in boxes like gifts, or put them in colorful sealed envelopes.)

When preteens arrive in class, say: **Today I have some unusual gifts for you. We're going to look at what they are and see how you might use them.**

Distribute the gifts, and have students open them. Then say: **Now get in a group with two or three other people and tell what gift you received.** Give students a

Leader Tip

You might want to write these questions on the board or on a sheet of newsprint so that everyone can see them.

minute to get in their groups and tell about their gifts. **Now in your group, discuss these two questions for each gift your group members received:**

- **How might you use this gift if you received it?**
- **How would this gift be of benefit to your group?**

After their discussions, have groups share highlights of what they discussed. Then say: **God gives us gifts that will help us serve him and others. Today we're going to be looking into how we can use those gifts.**

The Bible Experience

Same Attitude, Different Gifts

(For this activity you'll want to have a variety of creative presentation materials available. You may want to provide markers and poster board, modeling clay, a tape recorder, a video camera, costumes, a computer with PowerPoint, and any other such supplies you can make available.)

Form groups of four or five. Assign each group either Romans 12:1-3 or Romans 12:4-8. Have groups read their passages. Then say: **Your task is to decide what the main message of your passage is, and then to develop a way to teach that message to the rest of the class. You'll have fifteen minutes to prepare, and then you'll make your teaching presentation.**

Direct kids to the supplies available and let them get started. Roam from group to group, giving help where needed. After the fifteen minutes are up, have groups make their presentations. Then ask:

- **What does it mean to not "conform any longer to the pattern of this world"?**
- **What does it mean to "be transformed by the renewing of your mind"?**
- **What might be some signs that we think more highly of ourselves than we ought to?**
- **What does it mean that we're all members of one body in Christ?**

Say: **Now we're going to explore a bit more about what these gifts are.** Have kids form pairs. Assign each pair one or two of the "gifts" in Romans 12. If you used Choose Your Opening Option 2, you could assign them the "gifts" they were given then. Have pairs answer the following questions in relation to the gifts they are assigned:

- **If you had this gift, what would be some specific ways you could use this gift to serve God?**
- **How would the use of this gift be helpful to others in the church?**

Reflection and Application

Sticky Situations

(For this activity you will need copies of the "Sticky Situations" handout from page 104.)

Have preteens return to their groups of four or five. Distribute copies of the "Sticky Situations" handout. Assign each group one of the situations from the handout and have them prepare to role-play a response to each situation.

Allow several minutes for preparation, then have groups make their presentations. After they're finished, ask:

- **How did it feel to do these role-plays?**
- **How do you sometimes feel when you think about doing what God wants you to do?**
- **What can you learn from the thoughts you expressed in your role-plays?**
- **Why does God want us to properly use the gifts he's given us?**

Say: **God has given each of us gifts to use in serving him. God wants us to use those gifts to serve him and to help make the church better.**

Choose Your Closing

Option 1: My Gift From God

(For this activity you will not need any supplies.)

Say: **Since all Christians receive gifts from God, we can trust that each of us has at least one spiritual gift, and maybe several. We're going to take a few minutes now to think about what our spiritual gifts might be. I'm going to ask a few questions that I want you to think about. Don't answer them aloud. I'll give you a few moments to reflect on each question, then I'll close with prayer.**

Ask:
- **What special abilities do you think God has given you?**
- **What are you naturally able to do well, without trying very hard?**
- **How might you be able to use that ability for God?**
- **What will you do this week to begin seeking out opportunities to use your gift or gifts to serve God?**

Close your lesson with prayer, asking God to help your students discover and use the gifts he's given them.

Option 2: Where Can We Serve?

(For this activity you'll need a white board and marker, chalkboard and chalk, or newsprint and marker.)

Ask:
- **How can young people your age serve God in our church?**

Have students brainstorm several answers to this question, and list them on a white board or newsprint. Then ask:
- **How can young people your age serve God in our community?**

Again, have students brainstorm several answers, and list them on a white board or newsprint. Then say: **In a moment I'm going to close our session in prayer. I'd like for each of you to select one of these ways you can serve God. Pick one that fits what you think you'd like to do. That just might be an area in which God has given you a gift. As I pray, commit to following through on serving God in the way you've chosen. Your commitment will be just between you and God. God has given us all spiritual gifts, and he wants us to use them to serve him.**

Close your session in prayer, asking that God will help your students discover, develop, and use their gifts in serving him.

Sticky Situations

In your group, read your assigned situation and decide how you will role-play the interaction described at the end. Involve everyone in your group in the process. Then prepare to present your role-play.

Situation 1

Jenny is a friend of yours, but sometimes you can hardly stand her. She thinks her gift from God is her beautiful singing voice, and she's always ready to point out that she sings better than anyone else her age. She does have a beautiful voice, but she tends to look down on everyone else as if she's better than they are. One day she's at your house and blurts out, "Why do all the kids at church hate me?"

What can you share from this lesson that would be a help to Jenny?

Situation 2

You're in a drama group that's preparing a play to present to the adults in your church. Mike and a couple of other people created the whole play, and it's really good. However, Mike was left out when the leaders chose who would play each part. You felt sorry for him, but he really didn't do very well when he tried out. Mike's helping out with creating backgrounds for the play, which he also does very well, but after your drama meeting one day he says, "I sure wish I could be in the play. I guess I'm just not much good at anything!"

What can you share from this lesson that would be a help to Mike?

The Word in My Heart

Preteen kids most likely do not get excited about studying, except perhaps in a negative sense. They're learning to study in school, and that's a drag for many of them. They don't want to hear that they need to be studying the Bible as well, a book that many of them see as a dry old book that has little to do with their lives. However, this is a time in their lives when they're beginning to establish patterns that can last a lifetime. This is a great time for them to develop a pattern of regular Bible reading. And Bible reading doesn't have to be heavy study. You can remind kids that God wants to have a relationship—a friendship—with each of them. They talk to God through prayer; God talks to them (most often) through the Bible. Help kids understand that reading the Bible is the best way we have of getting to know God and learning what he wants to tell us. It's how we build a relationship with the creator of the universe!

Choose Your Opening

Option 1: Who's Your Hero?

(For this activity you will need note cards and pencils.)

When kids arrive, say: **We all have heroes. Some are imaginary characters we see on TV and in movies. Others are real-life people who may be celebrities, sports personalities, or family members.** Tell about one person who is or has been your hero. Then distribute note cards and pencils.

Say: **Right now, I want you to think of someone you'd consider your hero. On your note card, write down a list of things you know about that hero, but don't write down the hero's name. You might write down personality traits, special powers, occupation, or anything else you know about the hero.**

Give kids a couple of minutes to write about their heroes. Then collect the cards and redistribute them to kids randomly. Say: **If you get your own card back, it doesn't matter; just don't let anyone know.**

Form a circle, and have kids read the cards aloud one at a time. After each card is read, have kids guess who the hero is and also who wrote the card. If no one can guess the hero, have the writer of the card tell who it is. When all cards have been read, ask:

- **Why do you think we know so much about our heroes?**
- **How hard was it to guess who wrote each card?**
- **How do our heroes influence who we are?**

Say: **We get to know our heroes by watching them or reading about them or living with them. And that's the same way we can get to know God—by** watching him work in people's lives, by living with the Holy Spirit guiding us, and by reading about God in the Bible. Today we're going to look more at what we can gain by regularly reading God's Word.

Option 2: The Main Character

(For this activity, you'll need a variety of simple short stories. They can be children's books, or any other kind of story that will interest kids. No story should take less than two minutes or more than five minutes to read. Each story should include a main character the reader will learn about through the story. You'll also need a Bible.)

As kids arrive, give each one a short story. You might give early arrivers the longer stories. Tell kids to begin reading their stories whenever they want to. When all kids have arrived and read their stories, ask:

• **What did you think of coming to church and reading a story?**

• **What did you learn about the main character in your story?**

Allow a few volunteers to tell what they learned, but don't allow this question to take up more than a couple of minutes. Ask:

• **What would you know about your story's main character if you had never read the story? Explain.**

Hold up a Bible and say: **God is the main character in this story. It's a long story, and it takes a long time to read the whole thing. But we can learn little bits about God each time we read a portion of God's story. Today we're going to look at what we can gain from regularly studying God's Word.**

The Bible Experience

What Good Is It?

(For this activity you'll need paper, pencils, and Bibles.)

Say: **Today we're going to look at a portion of the Bible from 2 Timothy 3. As the Apostle Paul wrote this letter to Timothy, Paul was expecting to die very soon. Paul had led Timothy to faith in Jesus. In many ways Timothy was like a son to Paul. In this letter, Paul was passing along to Timothy the most important things to remember. Let's read 2 Timothy 3:14-17, then we're going to think about how important the Bible is for us today.**

Read the passage aloud, then distribute paper and pencils. Make sure everyone has a Bible. Say: **What we're going to do now is write letters telling someone else what's important about the Bible. Think of someone you know who doesn't know much about God or the Bible. Write a letter as if it were to that person, telling what he or she could gain from reading the Bible. Use thoughts from this Bible passage and put them into your own words. Your finished letter should echo the message Paul was expressing to Timothy, but relate it in your own words to today's situations.**

If kids have trouble understanding anything in the passage, give them help in understanding it. Don't make your suggestions too deeply theological, but keep them practical. When kids have completed their letters, have them read the letters aloud to the class. Applaud after each one and thank the child for the effort. If anyone doesn't want to read his or her letter, don't force the issue; allow that person to "pass." After all letters have been read, ask:

- **What's the biggest benefit of reading God's Word?**
- **If we actually sent these letters, what would the readers learn from them about us?**
- **How is this like learning about God by reading the Bible?**
- **How does getting to know God affect the things we do and say?**

Say: **Reading God's Word helps us in a lot of ways. Two of those ways are that it helps us get to know God and it helps us learn how to live. Those are both important things in a Christian's life.**

Reflection and Application

Getting to Know God

(For this activity you will not need any supplies.)

Say: **I'd like for you to think right now about someone from history that you know quite a bit about. It could be someone you've studied in school, or just someone you've learned about through reading on your own. Don't tell anyone who your character is.**

Give kids a minute to think, then say: **Now I'd like for you to mingle around the room, talking to others as if you're that person from history. For example, if you choose to be George Washington, you might say things such as, "I'm glad to meet you. I cannot tell a lie; I chopped down the cherry tree." Go from person to person saying as many different things as you can think of that your historical person might say.**

After about three minutes of mingling, or when kids seem to be running out of things to say, stop the activity. Then ask:

- **How easy was it to recognize the historical people others were portraying?**
- **How did you learn about your historical person?**
- **You seemed to know quite a lot about some of these people. Is knowing *about* someone the same as knowing them? Why or why not?**
- **How is the way we know God similar to the way we know these historical characters? How is it different?**
- **How does having a relationship with God change the way we know God?**
- **If you want to really build a relationship with someone, what do you have to do?**

Say: **To build a relationship with God, we have to spend time with him. As we get to know about God by reading the Bible, we can also develop our relationship with God, because that's the main way God speaks to us. As we talk to him in prayer and spend time in the Bible learning what God wants us to know about him, our relationship with God will grow. And more and more that relationship will positively affect the things we say and do.**

Option 1: What Do You Know?

(For this activity you will not need any supplies.)

Have kids think silently for a minute about the following questions:

- **What have you learned about God from the Bible?**
- **How has what you've learned about God helped you really get to know God?**
- **How has getting to know God helped your relationship with God grow?**
- **How has your relationship with God changed the things you say and do?**

After a time of reflection on the above questions, ask for volunteers to share their thoughts on any of the questions. Don't be uncomfortable with a few moments of silence. It may take a minute for kids to muster the courage to speak. But verbalizing their thoughts about their relationship with God will be good for them, and it will help you to know where they stand. Also, don't accept answers such as, "A lot" or "Not much." If kids give answers like that, ask them, "What do you mean by that?" or "Be more specific." Help them work through their own thoughts.

After at least a few have shared, say: **Spending time reading the Bible regularly doesn't mean hours every day. You might want to start out reading just a few verses. Just read until you hit something that speaks to you. The Gospel of John is a good place to start. Many people see that book as the center of God's message to us. You'll probably want to read an easy-to-read translation. Also, feel free to ask an older Christian you know if you're having trouble understanding something.**

Wrap up your class with prayer. Pray that kids will see the lasting benefits of building a relationship with God through the reading of God's Word.

Option 2: Meet the Author

(For this activity you will need one copy of the "Bible Reading Plan" handout on page 110 per student. You will also need Bibles in a variety of versions and translations.)

Say: **We've seen some pretty good reasons today for why we should read the greatest book ever written. The Bible is not only an awesome true story, God's love letter to us, and a great guide for how to live, but it is also the best way we have to get to know God.**

Some of you might be convinced that you should read the Bible, but you might not know quite how or where to start. Ask your students to look at their Bibles and check what version or translation they have. If they are not sure where to find this information, direct them to the cover, the spine, or the copyright pages in the front. Ask students to take turns telling what versions their Bibles are.

Say: **One good place to start Bible reading is to get a version that is easy to read. There are lots of good modern translations out, including several that are written specifically for children, youth, or students. Find one that you like, can easily read and understand, and feel comfortable with.**

Ask your students to share if they have any favorite Bible passages. Invite them to read their favorite passages aloud from their own Bibles or the Bibles you have brought, reading from a variety of versions and translations.

Say: **Once you have a Bible version you like, this is still a pretty big book. Where should you start? Should you just start at the beginning and plow your way through? Some people do read the Bible that way, but if you're just getting started, that can be pretty intimidating. Instead, you might want to start by concentrating on just one book at a time.**

Distribute the "Bible Reading Plan" handout, and say: **This handout gives you a suggestion of some passages you might want to use to get started reading the Bible. The passages are not very long, so try to read one each day. After only three weeks, you will have read the entire book of John! And by the end of the month, you will have finished three complete books of the Bible! By the end of forty days, you will have sampled five other books. There is nothing magical about this plan; it's just one way for you to get started and guide your reading, offering several passages that will help you get to know God better.**

Close class in prayer, thanking God for giving us his Word so we can get to know him better. Ask God to give your students the desire and the willpower to make Bible reading a regular habit, in their attempt to know him better.

Bible Reading Plan

Day 1: John 1

Day 2: John 2

Day 3: John 3

Day 4: John 4

Day 5: John 5

Day 6: John 6

Day 7: John 7

Day 8: John 8

Day 9: John 9

Day 10: John 10

Day 11: John 11

Day 12: John 12

Day 13: John 13

Day 14: John 14

Day 15: John 15

Day 16: John 16

Day 17: John 17

Day 18: John 18

Day 19: John 19

Day 20: John 20

Day 21: John 21

Day 22: 1 Corinthians 13

Day 23: Philippians 1

Day 24: Philippians 2

Day 25: Philippians 3

Day 26: Philippians 4

Day 27: James 1

Day 28: James 2

Day 29: James 3

Day 30: James 4

Day 31: James 5

Day 32: Matthew 5

Day 33: Matthew 6:25-34

Day 34: Matthew 7

Day 35: Ecclesiastes 3:1-14

Day 36: Psalm 8

Day 37: Psalm 37

Day 38: Psalm 51

Day 39: Psalm 139

Day 40: Isaiah 40:28-31; 43:1-3a

Days 41 and following: One chapter of Proverbs a day

Then ask some adults what their favorite books or passages are, and read them. Or venture out on your own!

Committed to Serve

Sharing My Faith

Preteen kids are often terrified of telling others about their faith. They fear rejection, and don't want to look foolish in front of their friends. Kind of like most adults! Part of the fear we all have is not knowing what to say—we don't have anything ready to say if the opportunity arises. This lesson will be a little different from most. Its focus is to help kids prepare to share their faith when God gives them a chance. You'll be spending most of your time in the Reflection and Application section, helping kids formulate something meaningful to say to get a conversation started about spiritual things.

Leader Tip

This lesson is designed for kids who already have a faith relationship with God through Jesus. If that's not the case for some of your kids, be sure to be sensitive to their needs.

Choose Your Opening

Option 1: Good News to Share

Say: **Pretend you're a medical scientist and you've just discovered a cure for heart disease. It doesn't hurt, and it will prolong the lives of all who suffer from heart disease.**

Ask:

• **Who would you want to tell about your discovery?**

• **Who would you want to be the first ones to take advantage of your new cure?**

• **How is this good news of a cure like the good news we have about Jesus?**

• **How is Jesus our cure for heart disease, spiritually speaking?**

• **Who do you want to tell about Jesus?**

Say: **If we really believe that our sins are forgiven and we can have a relationship with God by believing in Jesus, we will want to tell everyone we know—and especially those we really care about—what Jesus can do for them! Today we're going to prepare ourselves for doing that.**

Option 2: A Real Treat

(For this activity you'll need some kind of wrapped treat, such as candy bars or lunch cakes. Be sure to have enough for each student.)

Select two volunteers to be Sharers. Set out only a few of the treats. Say: **The two of you who are Sharers are to make sure everyone else has a treat. You may eat a treat yourself, but remember that your task is to make sure everyone else has one.**

If Sharers start breaking up the treats and passing out pieces, let that go on until they're finished. If Sharers ask you for more treats, give them to them. If Sharers give away the first treats, put out a few more, then later more, until everyone has one. When everyone has had at least part of a treat, ask:

- How did you feel about receiving a treat?
- Who would have gotten a treat if the Sharers had decided to be selfish and keep the treats for themselves?
- How is this like sharing the good news about Jesus with your friends?

Say: **For others to know about the good news of Jesus, we who already know him need to tell them. It's not always easy to share, but if we want them to know about Jesus, someone needs to tell them. We're going to be learning about how to do that today.**

The Bible Experience
· ·

Passing the Test

(For this activity you will need Bibles and copies of the "Chocolate Milk Instructions" handout from page 115. You'll also need a cup and spoon for each student, one-cup measuring cups, teaspoons, tablespoons, enough milk to give each student a cupful, and a supply of sugar and unsweetened baking cocoa. Place the unsweetened cocoa in an unmarked container. Keep all these items out of sight until you're ready for students to perform the "test.")

Say: **In a minute I'm going to give you a test. But first I want you to study what will be on the test.**

Distribute copies of the "Chocolate Milk Instructions" handout. Say: **Study this sheet so you know it well.**

Give kids a minute to study the sheet, then collect the sheets and get out the ingredients and utensils. Say: **Now here's the test. I'm going to see if you can do what the sheet said to do.**

Distribute the ingredients. You might want to have the sugar and unsweetened powdered chocolate in small resealable plastic bags so that one is available for every four or five kids. You might also want to have a helper pour the milk when the kids ask for it. Allow kids to enjoy their drinks when they have them ready. Then ask:
- **Were you able to pass the test?**
- **If not, why did something go wrong?**
- **If you had to make chocolate milk this way again at home, would you be able to do it?**

Have kids turn in their Bibles to 1 Peter 3:15, and ask a volunteer to read the verse aloud. Ask:
- **How is being prepared to "give the reason for the hope that you have" like being prepared to make chocolate milk this way? How is it different?**
- **How can we be prepared to tell others about Jesus?**

Say: **Now we're going to work on getting ready to tell others about the hope that we have in Jesus.**

Reflection and Application
· ·

My Jesus Story

(For this activity you will need paper, pencils, Bibles, copies of the "Important

Verses" handout from page 115, and newsprint or white board and marker, or chalk-board and chalk.)

Write the following list on a chalkboard, white board, or newsprint:

1. Life without Jesus
2. What happens when you have faith in Jesus
3. Life with Jesus

Distribute paper, pencils, and the "Important Verses" handout. Say: **You're each going to work on a simple presentation of what it means to follow Jesus. We're going to use this outline, and you will fill it in with statements from your own life and Bible verses of your own choosing. At the top of your paper, write, "My Jesus Story." Divide your paper into three sections and label them with the headings I've written here. Under "Life without Jesus," write one or two sentences about what it was like for you, or what you know it would be like, without Jesus. Then under "What happens when you have faith in Jesus," write one or two sentences about what you did and what changes took place when you made a faith commitment to Jesus. Under "Life with Jesus," write about how Jesus helps you now and the hope you have for the future because of him. Look up the Scripture verses on the "Important Verses" handout, and choose at least one to put with each section of your Jesus story.**

You may want to prepare your own simple "Jesus Story" in advance and read it to kids now as an example. Be sure it's not too perfect or complicated. Have kids work individually, but don't discourage them if they help each other. Go around the room helping those who have trouble. When kids are finished, have all who are willing read their stories to the class. Praise and applaud each one.

Say: **Now if you work on remembering what you put on these sheets, you'll "always be prepared to give an answer to everyone who asks you to give the reason for the hope that you have." And it's your own story that you can tell!**

Choose Your Closing

Option 1: Telling Our Stories

Have kids form pairs. To help solidify their stories in their minds, have each student tell his or her "Jesus Story" to his or her partner, looking at the paper only as much as needed. Encourage kids to read the Bible passages and tell their stories as if they were really telling them to someone who wanted to know about Jesus. When they're done, allow volunteers to tell what it was like telling their Jesus stories. Then close your class with prayer.

Option 2: Prayer Support

Have kids form groups of three or four. Encourage them to share in their groups someone they'd like a chance to tell about Jesus. Have kids avoid using names in their discussion. After each group member has shared, have kids pray together, asking God to help them be bold in telling others about what Jesus has done for them.

Chocolate Milk Instructions

You'll need:

1 cup milk

2 teaspoons baking cocoa

2 tablespoons sugar

Place the baking cocoa and the sugar in a cup. Thoroughly mix these two ingredients. Then stir in a few drops of milk and mix thoroughly until you have a paste-like substance. Then gradually stir in the rest of the milk.

Enjoy!

Important Verses

Choose from the following verses to help you explain what it means to follow Jesus:

John 3:16

John 14:6

Acts 16:31

Romans 3:23

Romans 5:7-8

Romans 6:23

1 John 1:9

13 Ways to Serve Others

Service Olympics

You can turn just about any service project into a fun preteen game by making it into a race. For example, if you want kids to pick up the trash around your area, make lists of trash items each group should pick up. Have kids race to see how many of the items on the list they can gather in the allotted time. (Don't forget gloves and bags before they go!)

The game idea also works for raking leaves: Use a large scale to weigh the bags at the end. You can have kids race to clean areas of the church. You might even try painting. (Don't forget dropcloths.) Who says work can't be fun?

Adopt-a-Whatever

Another great way to get preteens involved in service is to give them ownership and responsibility of the project. For example, if you want preteens to work on your church grounds or the grounds of a park or parking lot in your neighborhood, have them adopt a certain section.

Give kids the opportunity to plan out how they'll improve the area. Make sure you set a time frame for the adoption so kids don't have to take responsibility for the area forever. You'll be amazed at the initiative kids take and the ownership they'll have of the area.

Group Workcamp

If the kids in your group are heading off to junior high next year, consider taking your whole class to a Group Workcamp this summer. Group Workcamps are intensive one-week service mission trips. Workcamps offer you and your kids an opportunity to perform hands-on home-repair projects for needy families, many who have seen their homes damaged by natural disasters or years of can't-afford-to-fix disrepair. Group Workcamps will line up the worksites, materials, and evening programs. You just need to bring your kids with hearts ready to serve. Your kids must be at least twelve years old to participate. Go to www.groupworkcamps.com for more information.

Read On

Literacy is a gift that your preteens can share with the community. Call your local library to see if the kids from your group can volunteer to lead children in story time.

If that's not an option, connect with residential programs for adults and children with developmental disabilities. Ask if your preteens can read short stories to the residents.

Operation Elderly

Visiting a nursing home or a retirement home must be the number one suggested method of outreach in the church. There is a huge need in this area, and your preteen group can make this service mainstay exciting, fresh, and mission-minded.

Begin by telling preteens that you want to bring life and youth into the lives of people who may feel lonely and a little tired. Brainstorm with the kids to think of ways that your group can do that. Try to think about what the elderly in a retirement home or assisted living center want to do. For example, purchase some cheap board games such as backgammon and checkers, and play with residents. You can also prepare to push wheelchairs on walks through the grounds of the facility or lead residents in a hymn sing. (Contemporary worship doesn't usually go over too well in retirement homes, so stick with the oldies.) Other ideas include reading to the residents or performing a skit for them.

After you've developed a plan with the kids, call the activity coordinator at the facility you're targeting. Share your ideas with him or her. The coordinator will most likely be thrilled that you already have a plan and will work with you to make it happen.

After you've finalized your plans with the activity coordinator, have preteens form planning teams to accomplish each of the tasks necessary for the visit. Make sure you have accountability checks along the way for each group, and don't be afraid to ask parents for help where needed. Don't forget to secure permission slips from parents prior to the event.

Before you go, talk about your expectations with your preteens. Remind them of your goal and the importance of showing absolute respect for the residents. If kids separate during the outreach, make sure they are in pairs or trios, and that they know when and where they must return.

After the outreach, talk with your group about what they felt and saw. Ask them if they'd like to go again.

Prayer Walk

Target an area in your community that your preteens most want to see affected by the kingdom of God. If most of your kids go to one school, consider choosing that school for a prayer walk.

Begin by reading aloud the story of the battle of Jericho. Then explain that you believe God wants to "tear down the walls" at your targeted area. Set a date to walk around the facility and pray.

Secure the necessary permission slips, then meet with kids at the selected site. Your strategy for walking will depend on the size of the facility and of your group. You can either walk around the building once together, seven times together, or have trios stationed at various points around the building to circle the building relay-style.

Before you begin the walk, remind kids of your purpose, and encourage them to pray for specific people they know who visit the facility. Afterward, make sure you discuss the feelings and insights preteens had as they prayed.

Window Wash

Unfortunately, many adults have a negative view of preteens. They see them as destructive, violent, self-absorbed, and careless. Give your preteens a chance to prove those people wrong.

Buy squeegees, rags, and buckets for your kids to use. Target a neighborhood or business district for a window washing. Make sure kids stay in groups of at least three and that they respectfully ask homeowners and business operators before they start washing. Have kids wash the outside windows only.

Have adults inspect their work and make sure the groups stay together.

Sunday Breakfast

The pancake breakfast is no stranger to special church functions. But how many times have you given preteens the opportunity to serve breakfast to the Sunday school volunteers and children's ministry staff who have served them for so many years?

Plan with your preteens to serve breakfast to Sunday school teachers and children's ministry workers *before* Sunday school starts. Make sure you give kids as much responsibility in the planning and implementation as possible. Doing so is, of course, a bigger risk, but it also allows for a greater sense of accomplishment for the kids.

If you have a kitchen at your church, the details shouldn't be too hard to work out. If you don't have a kitchen, consider preparing toaster foods such as frozen waffles or toaster pastries. Or serve bagels, sweet rolls, fruit, and juice. If you have to purchase prepared foods, have kids set up tables and act as waiters so they can experience serving those who serve the children every week. Don't forget to send out plenty of reminders to the children's ministry workers to be there on time!

Baby-Sitting Service

Target a group in your church such as young marrieds or single moms for an evening of relief. Have parents bring their children to the church for a couple of hours of free baby-sitting. Make certain your preteens know what's expected of them, reminding them that the evening is not a time for play or socialization. And make sure you have enough adults available to offer support and direction to preteens.

For parents to feel comfortable, the baby-sitting area must be well-organized, clean, and safe. Assign one or two children to each preteen, and have preteens work to keep their assigned children safe and entertained. Make sure preteens don't go off on their own with the children. When parents return, have preteens give a full report on what their children did and how the time went.

Church History

Have the kids in your group serve the members of your congregation by creating a video documentary on the history of your church. Have kids interview longtime members about how the church was started, how it has changed, and future goals. Ask the pastor of your church for interesting records concerning the history of your church. Work together to edit the video, then present it to the congregation.

World Serve

Most preteens haven't yet bought into the cynical attitude that they can't make a difference. In fact, most preteens believe they can change the world. Talk with your kids about a global issue they'd like to help solve.

After you've decided on an issue, have kids search the Internet for organizations that can help them connect with people around the world. For example, if kids want to help with world hunger, your group could connect with World Vision.

If the organization doesn't have an easily accessible program, have kids e-mail or write to the organization, explaining what they hope to accomplish. Once you've decided on the program and approach, let kids go after it with all their hearts.

Where Does the Money Go?

Your preteens may have experienced fund-raisers to help the children's ministry or the youth ministry. This time, give them an opportunity to raise funds for a ministry in your church that they are not connected with. For example, have kids raise money for new nursery equipment or a vacation for the pastor.

Use the most proven methods of fund-raising in your church, such as a bake sale or car wash. Allow kids to present the money to the appropriate ministry in front of the entire congregation.

Side by Side

One of the best ways to build unity and relationship is to serve side by side. To help your kids see the body of Christ beyond just your church, arrange to have them work with another group of preteens from a different church in your community.

Meet a few times before the service project with the other group to plan the act of service. When kids go out to serve, make sure they are paired or grouped with people from the other church so relationships can be formed.

Group Publishing, Inc.
Attention: Product Development
P.O. Box 481
Loveland, CO 80539
Fax: (970) 679-4370

Evaluation for
No Miss Lessons for Preteen Kids 2

Please help Group Publishing, Inc. continue to provide innovative and useful resources for ministry. Please take a moment to fill out this evaluation and mail or fax it to us. Thanks!

● ● ●

1. As a whole, this book has been (circle one)

not very helpful   very helpful

1   2   3   4   5   6   7   8   9   10

2. The best things about this book:

3. Ways this book could be improved:

4. Things I will change because of this book:

5. Other books I'd like to see Group publish in the future:

6. Would you be interested in field-testing future Group products and giving us your feedback? If so, please fill in the information below:

Name _____

Church Name _____

Denomination _____ Church Size _____

Church Address _____

City _____ State _____ ZIP _____

Church Phone _____

E-mail _____